how to start a home-based

Jewelry Making Business

how to start a home-based

Jewelry Making Business

Maire Loughran

gpp®

Guilford, Connecticut

For my much-loved son, Joey, who serves his country aboard the USS *Harry S Truman*. I am prouder of you than mere words can ever describe.

Library of Congress Cataloging-in-Publication Data is available on file.

ISBN 978-0-7627-5012-2

Printed in the United States of America

10 9 8 7 6 5 4 3 2 1

Contents

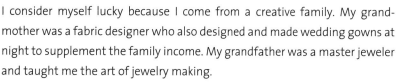

Introduction

I consider myself lucky because I come from a creative family. My grandmother was a fabric designer who also designed and made wedding gowns at night to supplement the family income. My grandfather was a master jeweler and taught me the art of jewelry making.

When I became an adult, this background in jewelry making encouraged me to do research on how to start and market a home-based business. I learned how to take high-resolution (high-res) images of jewelry, and how to write a press release and compelling copy about my pieces. Researching the history of jewelry, gemstones, and the life of jewelry designers was also very helpful. I became an expert on the various ethnic and ritual uses of jewelry.

Along the way I taught myself HTML code and got up to speed with Google Ad Sense and Ad Words, created a few different Web sites, including e-Commerce, and monetized with advertising. Once I felt my jewelry making skills were sufficient, I started entering juried schools, and moved from retail to wholesale marketing of my jewelry.

My home-based jewelry making goals haven't completely come to fruition—yet. Along with many other goals, I would like to gain acceptance into the juried Smithsonian Craft Show. I feel a good business is always a work in progress.

I went down a very meandering path with my jewelry making business. I had plenty of roadblocks thrown in my way, both self-created and beyond my control. The information contained in this book is the result of my years of creative and technical experience operating a home-based jewelry making business, including the practical business side, such as paying taxes and writing a business plan. Whether you want to run your business part-time to make some extra money, or quit your day job to make jewelry full-time, this book contains all the information you need to start and operate a successful home-based jewelry making business.

1 So You Want to Start Your Own Jewelry Making Business

You've probably purchased this book because you have made jewelry in the past for fun and now you want to turn your hobby into a profitable home-based business. If so, you are not alone. Over the past ten years, more and more people have been choosing self-employment to become their own boss, make more money, or have more-flexible hours.

Although no one can guarantee the success of any business, you *can* increase your chances of success by thoroughly researching and planning for your new jewelry making business before starting it. In this book, I will take you through the necessary steps to start your business. These are the same steps I took when starting my own successful home-based jewelry making business a few years ago. However, I've updated them to include all recent technological and marketing advances. Follow along with me through the next thirteen chapters as you start on the road to fulfilling your dream.

Hobby versus Business

Serious intent to make a livable profit is the most important divider between those who wish to pursue a hobby and those who are ready to start a business. Unless you are willing to take that big step to cross over from hobby to business, you are heading toward failure. Here are the questions you must ask yourself:

- Are you willing to put in the hours and effort needed to create a successful business?
- Do you intend to eventually live on or support other activities (leisure, retirement, education for the kids) with the profit from the business?
- Are you willing to change business methods and operations in order to move toward making a profit?

- Do you have practical experience in the art of jewelry making?
- Have you taken basic jewelry making educational classes?

I am not implying here that you can't start your home-based business on a part-time basis. In fact, most home-based businesses do start as part-time ventures. While some home-based business owners eventually quit their day jobs to work full-time in their own businesses, many do not. They meet their business objectives through running the business part-time only.

You may have young children at home, or maybe you've recently retired and just want to earn a little extra money each month. Just remember—whether it's part-time or full-time, you are wasting your time and money if you don't treat this business with serious intent. Establish financial goals and use your jewelry making business to achieve them.

If you're not planning to use your jewelry making business to put a roof over your head—a pretty strong motivating factor—keep in mind your personal goal. Let's say your goal is to pay cash for a new luxury vehicle. Each day when you start to work, keep that objective in mind. Push toward that objective as if you are working to make the mortgage payment on your house. If you go into the business with halfhearted effort, you'll end up with nothing.

What It Means to Be Self-Employed

If you tell someone you are self-employed, they immediately conjure up an image of being paid for fun. Like any other job you have ever had, being self-employed is hard work. This is true even in a more artistic field such as jewelry making. There are days when making jewelry is anything but fun. It's decidedly not fun to work twelve-hour days to get an important order out on schedule, or to have to work even when you're ill or have a death in the family.

The Demise of the Steady Paycheck

If you go at this full-on, quitting your day job, the biggest shock you'll have at the beginning is not receiving a regular paycheck. When you work for someone else, it's usually a certainty that you'll be receiving a check every regular payday. It's a big adjustment to not have that steady reliable income anymore. It's even more of an adjustment when you consider the employee benefits you may no longer have.

Procrastination

I've found that besides the money issue, the biggest impediment in moving a home-based business from infancy to success arises from not setting up a daily schedule. Once you head down that slippery slope of procrastination, it's hard to get back up the hill. I have worked out of my home for more than twenty years. I do not turn the television set on during normal business hours. I do not answer my personal telephone line unless I'm taking a break.

Here's what happens: A normal business task comes up that you don't particularly feel like doing. Maybe it's following up with a retail shop regarding the samples you dropped off last week. Sometimes you just hit a wall and can't come up with a jewelry design or exciting copy for your Web site. You figure you'll just do it later. Sometimes later turns into tomorrow or next week.

When you work for someone else, it's not an option to tell your boss you're just not in the mood. You have to get in the mood pretty darn quickly or the boss is going to be breathing down your neck. Too many similar episodes will have an effect on your raise or chances for promotion.

You need to treat every one of your jewelry making business tasks as if the most demanding boss you've ever had is going to be checking up on you and evaluating your performance. This is true, is it not? I know I am a lot harder on myself performance-wise than I have ever been with any of my employees.

I really hate making telephone calls. Even with the popular use of e-mail, when you are self-employed, some calls are unavoidable. My day goes a lot smoother when I just return or make all my telephone calls first thing in the morning. I get the task out of the way, and I feel good about moving forward with items that are more pleasurable on my to-do list. Keep that philosophy in mind. Do what you consider to be the hard stuff first each day, and your business will keep moving forward.

Persistence and Creativity

The opposite side of procrastination is persistence. No one is going to just throw money at you in the beginning simply because your jewelry designs are so fantastic. Persistence is the key. Okay, so maybe one store in your local area is not interested in carrying your jewelry designs. I'll bet there are hundreds more that you can approach. Perhaps the exact type of gemstone you want to use in a design is too costly or unavailable. Consider alternatives, buying in volume, or using a similarly colored stone.

Establish a Niche

Vivienne Chang is a certified crystal healer but has a very profitable sideline selling chakra-related jewelry. The jewelry is not elaborate by any means. She simply uses a knowledge base she already has and combines the appropriate gemstones, attaching them with jump rings to a linked bracelet or necklace. Obviously, some basic jewelry making and design skills are needed. She knows how to use a jump-ring tool and has an understanding of combining colors in an attractive fashion. We are not talking about some elaborate Cartier design here, but design that still fulfills her target market's jewelry need and generates revenue.

There will be days, many of them, when it will seem that problems are insurmountable. If it were easy to run a home-based business, everyone would do it. What will set you apart and eventually make your business a success is your dogged pursuit of getting the business up and running.

Flexibility is the cousin to persistence. It's foolhardy to continue with one business approach when you know it's just not working out. True persistence is when you are able to put mistakes behind you and concentrate your effort in another direction, with minimal hand wringing and regrets.

Another obstacle I guarantee you will encounter is trying to engage your creative side. This is a problem for some art school graduates. They have perfected the necessary techniques and can copy another's work almost flawlessly. However, when it comes to original designs, they are often flummoxed.

In many regards, either you have it or you don't. If you are not a truly creative individual, you can still make a good living with a home-based jewelry business. It's essential that you understand your limitations and work within those boundaries. For example, you can specialize in lower-priced jewelry for teens. It's not hard to track those trends, and the associated designs are relatively easy to create.

However, I believe you can kick-start creativity by keeping your eyes open and by looking to the familiar for inspiration. There is no substitute for research and hands-on work when it comes to inspiring creativity. Colors in nature are usually stunning and combine well in a piece of jewelry. Look through your supply catalogs for interesting new components. I skim through at least a hundred different types of periodicals each month, often finding jewelry making ideas in the weirdest places.

Take inspiration from Vivienne Chang, who sells chakra-related jewelry, and piggyback another skill into your creative jewelry making process. My father taught me to sew at a very young age. I enjoy putting my pieces of jewelry together using cold connections as if they were a sewing project, using wire for thread and jeweler's rivets to hold the pieces together. If you have training as a beautician, you can try braiding wire, then hammering and forming it into interesting necklace and bracelet shapes in much the same way that you create hairstyles.

Architectural Forms

If you have a background in architecture, even this very different field will have relevance when it comes to the creative jewelry making process. Architectural-style jewelry is set apart by the way it seems to be constructed like tiny machines or buildings. Checking out the details of this style of jewelry, you can imagine the blueprint behind the construction of the piece. Most architectural-style jewelry is very clean in appearance, with recognizable lines and forms.

One jewelry designer who employs this style is Kristine Bolhuis. Check out her architectural hinged jewelry on Ganoksin by accessing her page at www.ganoksin .com/eip04/16.htm.

Dealing with Customers

Yeah, they keep the door to your shop open, but at one point or another (and I say this tongue-in-cheek), all customers can be annoying. Your job as a business owner is to deal with your customers in a professional fashion no matter what the circumstance. The key is anticipating problems before they occur in order to keep customer complaints to a minimum. Anticipatory skills and customer care is your base for repeat customer business and customer referrals. There are three key areas to consider when addressing customer satisfaction—quality, punctuality, and businesslike demeanor.

Quality

Quality of the product, especially products arriving via mail order, is a major area of customer complaint. Most jewelry makers I know wear a design prototype for a few days to make sure it hangs correctly, that it's not going to fall apart, and that it is comfortable to wear. I've been known to throw my designs on a carpeted floor repeatedly to see if there are any undetected flaws in construction.

One of the major considerations when you are making repeated copies of the same jewelry design is the consistency aspect. If you are using a sample to sell jewelry, it is imperative that the products you send out are as close as possible to the model. Obviously, part of the appeal of handcrafted jewelry is the fact that each piece is unique. However, your finished goods do have to be very similar in appearance and quality of construction.

Punctuality

Do not overcommit yourself. If you take on more jobs than you are reasonably able to complete, it is a near certainty that something will go wrong. I once agreed to fulfill at the last minute an order for a wedding party of eight, when I knew that I only had enough chalcedony gemstones for six orders. I had two weeks to wrap up the order and didn't consider it a big deal to order more of the gemstone to finish the remaining two.

I placed an order with my gemstone supplier without a hitch and completed as much of the order as possible. Unfortunately, the chalcedony gemstones never arrived, and when I called the supplier, I found they had mistakenly shipped the order to my old address. A relatively simple order turned into a nightmare. Luckily, I was able to complete and ship the jewelry to the bride with a few days to spare. It was a major embarrassment for me and probably a great cause for concern on the part of the bride. Had this order been processed through a bridal shop that regularly referred work to me, it would have been a disaster.

If your customer needs an order by a certain day, make sure you make delivery the day before. When I accepted orders through my e-commerce Web site, I had a policy of two weeks for order fulfillment—longer during the holiday season. Once you start hiring jewelry making apprentices, a topic I discuss in chapter 12, order fulfillment can be timelier. For now, you want to put out a quality piece and build your reputation as such.

Businesslike Demeanor

It is normally not a good idea to have too friendly of a relationship with any major customer. Have you ever heard the old adage "Familiarity breeds contempt"? I never allow a major customer to know too much about my personal life. When my husband died, a few business acquaintances saw the notice in the local newspaper. They were surprised to learn that not only was I married, but I also had a child.

Similarly, you should never be out of the office on vacation. You're always either on a buying trip, meeting with out-of-town customers, or attending a trade show. Too many trips to Europe or Hawaii and the customer will start thinking they are paying too much for your product. I'm not joking. An acquaintance of mine had a customer tell her exactly that after she'd returned from a two-day weekend skiing in Aspen—her first vacation in over a year.

It also seems to be a perverse facet of human nature that if a customer knows you have personal events pending, they will almost always manufacture an emergency in a subconscious attempt to throw a monkey wrench into your plans. Ironically, you'll probably find your smaller customers are more prone to this type of behavior.

Additionally, some customers will try to take advantage of a friendly relationship by asking for discounts or by being late in paying your invoices. Nip this in the bud by adopting a professional yet approachable demeanor with all your customers.

Support from Family

Every home-based business ultimately turns into a family effort. Make this a positive element rather than a negative one by emphasizing to all family members the eventual benefits that will come from the home-based business.

Your spouse and kids may be gung-ho on the idea until you sequester yourself in your workroom after dinner to finish a project. Carving out business time that is respected by the other members in your family will be an ongoing issue. I found that setting reasonable regular business hours and having a strict enforcement policy is a big help. If your family knows you work each day from 4:00 p.m. to 7:00 p.m., most families will eventually realize it's important to put noncritical issues on hold during those three hours.

Getting started each morning at your home-based business is no less serious than getting on a commuter train to go to a job in the city. Therefore, I don't consider working at home to be a substitute for child-care arrangements. It will be impossible for you to concentrate if you are interrupted every fifteen minutes on one pretense or another.

Ideally, if you are the household's primary child-care provider, your children are in school. That gives you a nice block of time each day to work between school drop-off and pickup. If your children aren't of kindergarten age, you might consider placing your child in day care two or three days a week and concentrating your work efforts to those two or three days. Think about forming a child-care cooperative with two or three trusted neighbors or friends. You can rotate child care and have a few free days a week to work.

Knowing When to Quit

It is also important to know when to pack it up for the day and quit. This can be difficult when your workshop is in your home. You'll probably find that you work harder and longer hours than you ever did for an outside employer.

However, you should have an established routine to end the day just as you probably have when working for someone else. I find that making a to-do list at the end of each day allows me to wind down. If I have the next day organized, I find it's also easier to stop thinking about those pending issues. Once you close that workroom door for the evening, make sure you also move completely into your nonwork mode.

Required Skill Set for a Jewelry Making Business

Practical Experience

People who want to know how to start a jewelry making business often e-mail me to ask about the best way to start their business. I'm often amazed by how many of them have yet to make a single piece of jewelry. Outside of the basic design process, they have no practical jewelry making experience.

It's impossible to start any type of business unless you have sufficient practical experience. This fact isn't any truer for a dentist or plumber than it is for a jewelry maker. You can't just wake up one day, draw a few sketches, and decide that you're going to open a business selling handcrafted jewelry. Waking up and drawing the sketches is the first step. Developing well-honed techniques from hours of experience is your next step, prior to announcing yourself to the world as a serious businessperson.

If you are reading this chapter and you don't have sufficient practical experience, jump ahead to chapter 13. In this chapter, I discuss jewelry making training and certification. Select a training method and get started taking classes. As you hone your creative skills, work your way through the rest of the book to find out about the practical business, tax, and marketing skills. Both sides of your brain will meet up at the end and you'll be ready to make your home-based jewelry making dream a reality.

Taking a Design from Idea to Completion

Conceptual jewelry ideas can come from many different inspirations. Maybe you had occasion to purchase a large lot of beautiful Australian opal doublets and you are going to design around the gemstone. Could be a large retail customer needs matching pearl necklaces and bracelets. Perhaps you are free-associating, sketching out designs and matching the gemstone and metal details as the design ideas come to life.

As your career develops, all of the above circumstances can certainly happen. What ties your design processes together is the fact that you must carry your idea from conception to completion in a quality fashion.

Everyone has different abilities, and, based on right- or left-brain dominance, different ways of approaching their design process. I'm not that great of a sketcher. My design sketchbook, a chapter 2 topic, is filled with doodles and detailed notes rather than exact line drawings. I envy those designers who are able to draw a detailed sketch of a design. However, it's equally as important to be able to bring that sketch to fruition.

If bringing your sketch to completion is a step that evades you, repetitive practice making jewelry will certainly help. Keep in mind that some jewelry making techniques will just naturally be easier for you than others. If you want to construct jewelry using unfamiliar techniques that you can't master on your own, consider taking some continuing education courses in those areas.

Left-Brain versus Right-Brain Characteristics

Everyone has one side of their brain that is dominant. You tend to process information using your dominant side. Knowing which of your brain hemispheres is dominant will help you figure out the best approach to starting your jewelry making business.

Left Brain	Right Brain
You learn by listening; you perform very well in lecture-based classes._____	You learn by watching and doing; you perform very well in lab-based classes._____
Problem solving is logical. You work from point A to B to C until a solution is reached._____	Problem solving is intuitive based upon instinct rather than logic. You may start at the middle and work forward or backward to arrive at a solution._____
You compare alternatives by looking at their differences._____	You compare alternatives by looking at their similarities._____
You plan events down to the last detail. For example, you'll have all hotel reservations made well in advance of a trip._____	You're spontaneous and leave details open to chance. For example, you'll book a suitable hotel room after arriving at the destination._____
You prefer talking and writing._____	You prefer drawing and designing._____
You prefer multiple-choice tests._____	You prefer tests with open-ended essay questions._____
You like to follow the rules without deviation._____	You prefer to bend the rules to adjust them to your particular circumstances._____
Your work area is neat and organized._____	Your work area is chaotic but you know where everything is._____
One task at a time is worked on from start to finish._____	You jump back and forth between different tasks._____
If you make a purchase where assembly is required, you work through the instructions step by step._____	If you make a purchase where assembly is required, you look at the picture on the box and try to figure out how the pieces fit together without reading the instructions._____
If you get lost while driving, you stop to ask for directions or take a closer look at a map._____	If you get lost while driving, you keep driving until something looks familiar or another occupant of the car forces you to stop._____
You make few decisions based upon hunches._____	Many of your decisions are based upon what feels "right."_____
You are punctual for most engagements._____	You have the reputation of always being the last person to arrive at an event._____
You explain with words._____	You accompany speech with gestures._____
Ideas are formed while sitting up at your desk. _____	Ideas are formed when laying down. Sometimes you'll wake up after a night's rest knowing exactly how to solve a problem._____
Guarded personality_____	Open personality_____

Evaluating your answers: If they indicate mostly left-brain dominance, you may feel that a creative-type business such as jewelry making is not a good fit for you. This is not true. What it means is that you will need to pay more attention to right-brain-type techniques for the creative jewelry making tasks. Your left-brain dominance will be an asset while handling the nuts-and-bolts business details.

Quality of Construction

There is no substitute for quality. It doesn't matter how lustrous the gemstone or unique the design, if your piece is difficult or painful to wear or just flat out falls apart, you have no business selling jewelry. Keep in mind that unrelated third parties will expect much higher quality in your work than the family members and friends that you made jewelry for in the past.

I cannot emphasize this enough: Practice and repetition are the keys to quality design. Remember, no one is perfect. Even with years of practice, you will occasionally have to jettison a partially made piece of jewelry because something went horribly wrong in the fabrication process. This is normal. Salvage what raw materials you can and start again. Regardless of price, never let a piece of jewelry leave your workshop that you aren't proud of.

Designing for Others

To be successful you often have to create designs and use materials other than those you prefer. Even within your target market, everyone is different. You have to offer a wide array of styles and designs to maximize your sales.

I personally don't like to wear bracelets; I find them annoying. Based on my personal preference, if I were to make only necklaces and earrings, I would be reducing my potential customer base by one-third. Not good. Then I would have to create an artificial demand to sell more necklaces and earrings rather than reaping the benefit of the naturally occurring demand for bracelets.

Develop a Thick Skin

Self-Promoting

Many business owners find it difficult to self-promote. I think this hearkens back to when we were children and were told it wasn't polite to boast. If you're not going to sing the praises of your business, who is? It's not obnoxious bragging to be self-promoting; it's just good business sense.

The best way to self-promote is to always be wearing a piece of your jewelry. When you are complimented on it, acknowledge that it is self-designed. Take it one step further and ask if the person is interested in buying the same piece. Quote a price, state a delivery date, and hand them a card. Seems a little too pushy? It will be slightly awkward at first for all but the most outgoing in nature.

However, how many times have you been asked where you purchased a certain item of clothing or who cut and colors your hair? Did you feel weird giving out that information? Promoting your own jewelry designs is no different.

Accepting Criticism

It would be a pretty boring world if we all had the same opinion. Not everyone is going to fall in love with your jewelry designs. Keep in mind that some criticism is productive, and that some people will criticize merely because they are jealous. Learn how to differentiate between the two types and develop a thick skin.

Factors to Consider When You Bring a Design to Market

I asked a popular online vendor, The Orchid Boutique, what criteria they use when selecting jewelry to sell on their Web site. Two major factors in moving a design idea to completion are price and that intangible "feel good" aspect behind each purchase. Here's their philosophy on both.

"Price plays less of a [role] in jewelry than it does on clothing. Jewelry, for the most part, has the unique quality of a universal fit, unlike clothing articles. A size 10 woman with a colorful and original piece of jewelry stands out just as a much as a size-2 woman. That gives jewelry a competitive advantage over other accessory items. We have been taught that a fine piece such as a necklace, bracelet, or pair of earrings embellishes/enhances/dresses up your attire. It's a wish fulfillment fantasy combined with a fashion statement. In sum, while price may influence some buyers it is not the top determinator in the popularity of a jewelry piece."

Go to www.theorchidboutique.com and select Jewelry from the horizontal toolbar at the top of their home page to check out how they apply these concepts to their selection of jewelry retailing on their site.

I have covered the basics of how to transform your jewelry making hobby into a revenue-producing business. In the next chapter, I talk more specifically about what you need to do to get started.

2

From Dreams to Reality: Defining Your Jewelry Making Business

What You'll Need to Get Started

Now is the time to isolate and deal with the three major areas of concern prior to making the switch from hobbyist to professional jewelry maker. You've probably guessed that one area of concern is money. The other two are setting up your physical work area and defining your target market.

Work and Storage Space

Do you have adequate work space and storage space for your business? I further elaborate on how to set up your work space in chapter 3. For now, your job is to take a good look around your home and figure out where you will work.

You may already have a work space set aside for your hobby. Is it large enough to do the amount of work that you will need to do once you ramp up your business? If it isn't, what about your garage or basement? Can you rearrange those areas into a work space?

Storage for a serious part- or full-time jewelry making business will vary depending on your area of interest. Beading takes up less space than metalwork and many of the other jewelry making disciplines. However, even those who bead will need storage space to organize the different beads, beading wire, connections, and clasps into a logical system.

Time is money, and if you are constantly searching for the right component, you have lost money. Ditto purchasing in volume. Purchasing more than a few components at a time saves money. However, you need to have a place to store these extra raw materials.

Define Your Target Market

It's extremely important to have a good idea as to the nature of your target market. It's not sufficient to isolate females or males. This is too broad a group. Do you want to design jewelry for under-35 females? Maybe your target market is bridal, any age group. Alternatively, body jewelry. Narrow it down, and as you build your business, increase the scope if you desire.

Looking Ahead: Is it Necessary to Increase Your Scope?

Increasing the scope of your business may not be a step you'll ever take. I have a friend who owns a body-piercing jewelry business. That is all she makes. Each piece of jewelry retails for less than $15. However, because of the volume of her sales, she was a millionaire in just a few years.

I have another friend who owns a lapel pin business. This really hovers on the fine line between jewelry and business marketing. However, he has not expanded his business any further—and he's also a millionaire.
It can be done. You can do it.

Defining and narrowing your target market initially allows you to focus yourself. The worst thing a new business owner can do is fly all over the map. Focus and serve your target market with a well-made product at a reasonable price.

It's important to define your target market so you can estimate the cost of your start-up expenses. More small businesses fail because of undercapitalization than for any other reason. If you don't have sufficient sources of ready cash for your start-up expenses, you're not going to be able to cover future operating expenses. If this is the case, it's time to take a step back and figure out a solution.

The solution might be to add to your savings account before you go into this full force. Perhaps you can absorb into your budget the periodic payment on borrowed funds. Another consideration is to take on a partner or investor. Although this would be my least-desired option, it might work for you. This topic is covered in more detail in chapter 12.

Estimated Start-Up Expenses

Put together as detailed a list as you can of all the expenses you anticipate for your business. These can include business licenses, auto expenses, business cards, a printer and/or scanner, software, digital camera, subscriptions to trade periodicals, jewelry making tools and supplies, Internet access, advertising, basic office and mailing supplies, and so forth. This list will help you determine how much money you'll need up front to start your business.

Define Your Work Style

Next, do an honest analysis of how you like to work. Everyone is different. Knowing your work-style preferences increases the likelihood of your business success, and it will definitely increase your job satisfaction.

Part-Time versus Full-Time

You need to decide if you are going to pursue your jewelry making business full- or part-time. If you already have a full-time job and you plan to quit, this is a decision that you make only after much soul searching and analysis of your cash ins and outs.

Unless you have signed customer contracts in place, you probably won't make enough cash to support yourself for at least the first year. But everyone is different. Maybe your spouse has sufficient income. Perhaps you have just won the lottery or received an inheritance. Different life events will affect your decision.

Day Person versus Night

While making jewelry lends itself to daytime work, using natural light, many people aren't "day" people. I've known a few; they only come alive in the late afternoon. On the other hand, maybe you're at your best in the early morning and start to slow down after lunch.

I prefer to work on my designs early in the morning when I am fresh, and place orders and read trade periodicals later in the day. Consider what type of person you are, isolate when you are the most productive, and do the heavy lifting of the jewelry making business during those hours.

Beginning Part-Time Is Typical

Most small business owners I know, myself included, started their first small business on a part-time basis. For example, I have friends with a very successful retail jewelry shop. In the beginning, they both had full-time jobs—the wife as a dental hygienist, and the husband, a high school teacher.

Every day after work they started their second shift, making jewelry. Eventually they moved their home-based business into a retail shop, still keeping their day jobs. The shop was only open from 4:00 p.m. to 8:00 p.m. weekdays, with normal retail hours on the weekends.

Initially, they covered all the shop hours themselves, with some part-time help on the weekends. Eight months later, they were able to quit their day jobs. Ten years later, it is still a thriving business, now with ten employees. Hard work in the beginning pays off in time.

Work Methods

Personality traits affect how we handle tasks across the board, not just in the business world. Look back to how you preferred to study in school. Some people need complete peace and quiet. I had college roommates who could only study while the radio and television were going full blast. Others learn best by doing, and for some, it's a combination of book knowledge and hands-on work.

Maybe you're the type of person who likes to tackle a task and finish it in one session. Others like to break their work up into pieces, with frequent short breaks. If you've ever worked in an office, you are familiar with the cube rats—those employees that scurry around the work space, chitchatting. As annoying as this is to their victims, it's their way of being productive—or nonproductive as the case might be—but you get the general idea.

You're the boss now. Figure out your personality type and run with it. Knowing how you best like to work will certainly increase your productivity. The fact is, you're the main beneficiary of your efforts now.

Types of Jewelry Making Approaches

When first starting out, it's important to offer a range of jewelry, while still special-izing within that range. Keeping to one basic concept serves to minimize the cost of your goods and allows you to focus. For example, you may like to work with sterling silver. Keep to that one design vision in the beginning.

Ideally, you'll build up brand recognition using that type of metal. You can always expand your line in the future and add karated gold or base metals to your skill set.

Brand Recognition at Work

Todd Reed's work is a great example of specialization. You cannot pick up a jewelry trade publication without seeing his name mentioned in a complimentary fashion by those working in the industry. He is a perpetual favorite at all the fine art jewelry competitions he enters. This translates into customer sales.

He has expanded somewhat now, but his design aesthetic for many years was working with raw diamonds and 18K gold. By concentrating on this design style and producing a stellar product, he successfully branded himself. While others also work with raw diamonds, his name is synonymous with the medium in the industry, and, more important from a customer standpoint, in the press. See what I mean by checking out his awesome designs at www.toddreed.com.

Limited Runs

If you're using a specific type of gemstone or component, you may be forced into doing limited runs. It's a little disconcerting to buy a raw material from a vendor for months only to see them abruptly discontinue it. There's also the potential the ven-dor may raise the price of the raw material so high that you can no longer effectively sell your product.

This happened to me with blue topaz a few years ago. The size and shape bead I was using disappeared from the market. This was also the year that blue topaz was named the second most popular blue gemstone, a contributing factor.

Every jewelry maker does limited runs to a certain degree. Your job satisfaction plays into this equation. After a while, you may simply decide that you don't want to make a certain design anymore.

Additionally, in time, the design may become dated or the market saturated with like product. One exception to this rule is Tiffany & Co. designer Elsa Peretti. Her Diamonds by the Yard© and Round Pendant have been marketed at Tiffany for years.

The Round Pendant has changed somewhat over the years with the use of different materials. Recently, Elsa Peretti introduced a pavé diamond Round Pendant. The basic concept remains the same: round pendant with her signature dimple hung on a silk cord.

Check out the Elsa Peretti collection at Tiffany & Co.'s Web site (www.tiffany.com). Here is another jewelry artist who has branded herself with the use of materials, technique, and design. None of her designs is that elaborate or unique; nonetheless, she's made them her own through consistency of design style.

Additionally, many of her designs aren't even that hard to make. I have a series of articles in my Feature Jewelry column at www.suite101.com detailing how to duplicate the Round Pendant in sterling silver. The first one took me less than one hour to make, and I believe the components cost less than $15 retail. At that time, the Round Pendant was retailing for $450.

One-of-a-Kind Artisan Pieces

Based upon your target market, you may prefer to make only one of each jewelry design. Many jewelry artists do this if the gemstone in the piece is unique or if the design is such that it cannot be re-created exactly.

If you plan to enter juried shows, you must create a few one-of-a-kind pieces. Your ordinary day-to-day jewelry designs aren't going to get you into these shows. Most jurors like to see jewelry designs with flair. After acceptance, you offer a range of styles and prices at the show. Just make sure you stay within the confines of what you said you would present at the show. If you attempt to sell items the show organizers feel are inappropriate, you may be asked to leave the show.

Some jewelry images used to promote shows to the public are extremely ornate and overcomplicated. You might wonder what type of occasion warrants such a piece of jewelry. It's the same theory used for the clothing styles that come down the runways: Show the best of the best and then rework the design and materials for ready-to-wear.

Commission Work

You may have already done commission work without knowing it. A friend or coworker admires a piece of jewelry and asks you to re-create it, but working to their specifications. This type of jewelry design requires a special attitude, as you have to carry out what the customer wants by working with their vision rather than your own.

Take care that you don't accept commissioned work requiring a skill, knowledge, or material with which you are not familiar. Now is not the time to hone your technique in soldering or stone setting.

Before beginning, make sure you have a meeting of the minds with your customer as to the design, cost, and materials for the project at hand. Depending on the price, this could be verbal or in writing. Collect a deposit covering at least the cost of your raw materials. This gauges your customer's interest and decreases the possibility that your customer will walk away from the commission when you are ready to make delivery.

Production-Line Jewelry

If you're going to be making many pieces of the same design, it's best to set up the whole operation production-line style. Using Elsa Peretti's Round Pendant as an example, here is how I would set up the production line for this piece of jewelry:

- Purchase 100 round sterling silver forms for the pendant base and 100 black silk cords with an attached clasp.
- Drill a small hole at the top of each form to insert the black silk cord.
- Place each form into a dapping block to create the concave shape. Dapping blocks are made from wood or metal and are used to shape jewelry sheet or forms in a concave shape. This is done by placing the metal into the cup formed in the block and striking it with a mallet to alter its shape.
- Reverse each form in the dapping block and punch to create the dimple.
- Attach the black silk cord to each finished pendant.

I've left out a few steps, such as polishing and checking the edges. However, you get the main idea—which is, you don't make each pendant from start to finish individually. All 100 pendants go through the same production step before you move on to the next step.

The jewelry making process is efficient and quick. However, with production-line pieces, I feel a bit of the creative joy is removed from the whole process. I prefer to come up with the design, refine it, test a prototype, and hire workers to run the pieces through the production line, paying each employee by the piece.

Fine, Bridge, and Costume Jewelry

It's best in the beginning to limit your design style to a particular type of jewelry. There are three: fine, bridge, and costume, and here is a thumbnail sketch of each type:

Fine Jewelry

The main characteristic of this jewelry is the use of precious metals, such as kara-ted gold and platinum. If set with gemstones, usually only the precious gemstones (ruby, sapphire, emerald, or diamond) will qualify the piece to be designated as fine. Cartier comes to mind as one quite famous classic fine jewelry designer.

Bridge Jewelry

This type of jewelry gets its name from the fact that it is the bridge between fine and costume jewelry. This type is also made of precious metals, usually sterling silver. Aquamarine, garnet, citrine, and amethyst are examples of semiprecious gemstones used in bridge jewelry. Basically, any gemstone that is not one of the ones listed under fine is considered semiprecious.

Just a word here on the quality of gemstones: A poorly cut, bad specimen of ruby can be worth much less than an excellent specimen of, say, topaz or opal. So while ruby, emerald, and sapphire are the three precious colored gemstones, joined by diamond, it does not always follow that jewelry set with these gemstones is considered fine. A jeweler will typically not waste the money to use karated gold to set an inferior precious gemstone, although it does happen.

Costume Jewelry

Costume jewelry is made with base metals that are gold, rhodium, or silver plate. It is normally set with faceted glass stones such as rhinestones or crystals. This term to describe non-precious jewelry came into popular use in the 1930s when coined by movie producer Cecil B. DeMille.

If costume jewelry is your area of interest, check out the work of two highly regarded costume jewelry designers, Monet and Kenneth Jay Lane. Both have fabulous pieces of jewelry retailing at under $50. Their work provides a benchmark as to the quality you should be achieving if making costume jewelry.

Monet

Monet started in 1937 as an offshoot of a company that produced metal art deco monograms for purses. Monet's initial goal was to create elegant yet affordable women's jewelry. To add that special touch to their line, Monet was the first costume design house to stamp their trade name into every piece of jewelry.

Monet has remained popular since then and is available for sale in just about every department store in the United States and Canada. Clothing designer Liz Claiborne has a fabulous Monet line that includes gold- and silver-plated jewelry set with coral, common green opal, and blue, pink, and green crystals.

Kenneth Jay Lane

One of Kenneth Jay Lane's most famous customers is former United States First Lady Barbara Bush. He was the designer of her signature three-strand pearl necklace. In business for more than forty years, vintage Kenneth Jay Lane jewelry is very popular and expensive. The company is still in existence, marketing its contemporaneous jewelry designs in many different outlets.

Lane graduated from the world-famous Rhode Island School of Design (RISD) and made his start by designing shoes prior to designing jewelry. Some truly gorgeous pieces of Kenneth Jay Lane jewelry are available from online and television mega-shopping venue QVC. As Kenneth Jay Lane states in his book, *Kenneth Jay Lane: Faking It,* his goal is "creating affordable, beautiful jewelry." This will be your mission as well if you decide to work in the costume jewelry field.

Working Seasonally

One can make a reasonably good living in the jewelry making trade working seasonally. If you really market yourself and get your name out there, you can do much better than just reasonably well.

Weddings

Wedding jewelry is a fantastic potential source of cash. People do get married year-round. However, there are certain times of year that are the most popular for weddings (this can vary depending on the region).

If wedding jewelry is an area of interest to you, the best plan of attack is to introduce yourself to local wedding planners and bridal shops. Scrutinize bridal magazines looking for trends in design. Look to the queen of wedding gown design, Vera Wang, to see what direction her collection is taking for the season, and design your jewelry around it.

Prom

Although proms take place in the spring, this big event in the life of teens has more than likely been the focal point of many a conversation since January. The absolute worst is arriving at prom only to see that someone else is wearing the same dress. It doesn't matter who looks better in the dress, it's still a major catastrophe.

Allowing for this, most young women attending prom have tied down their choice of gown by March. Prom jewelry sales start increasing at the same time, through the end of April. Have your prom line of jewelry ready to go in January.

Year-End Holidays

In my experience, whether the celebration is Christmas, Hanukkah, Kwanzaa, or some other event, holiday sales start increasing a week before Thanksgiving and are strong through the last week of December.

I have a friend who owns an advertising agency. Fourth-quarter sales of advertising for all media start firming up in the second quarter; that's how important the holiday season is to retailers. A good holiday season can carry a retailer for the rest of the year.

Your objective if you plan to sell seasonally is to track the trends and know what clothing designers will be pushing so that your jewelry will coordinate with upcoming styles. You don't need a crystal ball to do this. Keep on top of the fashions coming down the runway at Fashion Week and plan your jewelry line accordingly. Also, keep an eye on the Pantone Fashion Color Reports. Pantone, Inc. is the world-renowned authority on color. If they say a color will be popular for spring 2010, it *will* be popular.

Keep An Eye on Fashion Week

Fashion Week, which occurs in different cities worldwide for each season, takes place months before the relevant season. For example, Fall Fashion Week takes place in the early spring of each year.

A good way to keep current on the fashions coming down the runways is to sign up for the www.style.com Fashion Flash. You'll receive at least weekly updates on what's happening in the fashion world that will help shape the direction of your seasonal collection.

Special Requirements of Jewelry Making Techniques

As you're walking through the steps to turn your dream into a reality, consider unique tools and requirements for the type of jewelry making techniques you plan to employ in your business. The type of techniques you employ will directly influence your start-up costs.

Precious Metal Clay

The big issue with precious metal clay is firing it. Some use a butane torch similar to what cooks use to make crème brûlée. Depending on the size of your work, this may not be a feasible option. It's also very time-consuming. Most professionals purchase a kiln to fire their work.

A kiln takes up a fair amount of space and needs to be placed in a secure location. Read the safety instructions for your kiln and find an appropriate place in your home for setup.

Polymer Clay

This jewelry making technique adapts itself to the kitchen quite well, as you can bake polymer clay in a 325-degree oven. If you don't wish to condition the clay by hand, you can use a clay-dedicated pasta machine, which takes up little space as well. Just make sure that this particular pasta machine is labeled as such. Your only other work-space issue is the fact that clay damages wood surfaces. Most polymer clay artists work on a ceramic tile and use the same tile to bake the piece in the oven.

Beading

Many jewelry artists start out as beaders since the tools are relatively inexpensive and this jewelry making technique does not require the use of a kiln or torch.

However, don't downplay the appeal of beads. The history of beads goes back to prehistoric times. Beads are used not just for adornment but also as talismans, status symbols, and religious articles. Those beaders who advance beyond the basic skills make their own beads using other jewelry making disciplines, such as polymer and precious metal clay or lampwork glass beads.

If you plan to knot your beading thread between beads, one piece of specialty equipment I highly recommend is a bead knotter. My first knotter cost almost $50. Luckily, they have dramatically decreased in price. You should be able to find one for less than $20.

Most bead knotters work using the same basic steps. You'll be able to knot pearls and beads professionally and quickly. They can be used with silk or nylon bead cord. They're a little tricky to use at first, but once you get the hang of it, you can potentially knot up to five beads per second.

Silversmithing

This is my preferred area of jewelry design. Silversmiths work the metal with special hammers and forms connecting the parts either using cold connections or a torch to solder the pieces together.

It is possible to create elaborate, wonderful designs using only cold connections such as rivets, staples, and glue. If you prefer to use a torch, the same caveat applies as with a kiln. Make sure you have a safe place to operate your torch. Using a torch, you have the additional issue of accidentally setting your work space on fire.

I recommend being completely up to speed on how to use a torch prior to introducing one into your home. Many teaching museums and trade schools have continuing education classes on this topic.

Wirework

The popularity of wirework runs a close second to beadwork for beginning jewelry artists. Wirework is actually an offshoot of cold connections, as gemstones and other objects are attached to the piece of jewelry using only the wirework wrapping technique.

Your main pieces of equipment are pliers and cutters. Many wirework artists prefer to work with one gauge and style wire for the construction and one for the wrapping. Coils of wire take up little space. If you work in sterling silver, just make sure your wire is stored with anti-tarnish strips that you change frequently.

Other Precious and Base Metals

If you plan to work with other metals, such as karated gold, copper, or stainless steel, the same basics apply. Your main area of concern is to make sure you are using the appropriate temperature when soldering these metals.

Green Jewelry

This term applies to using recycled or renewable raw materials. This runs the gamut of recycling your sterling silver and karated gold scraps to using found items. Some examples of found items are recycled record albums, billboard media, coins, rusty nails, and orphan jewelry sets found at thrift stores. This market is wide open; whatever you can find to make into an attractive piece of jewelry is fair game.

Green Jewelry at Work

Fiddlehead Studio, a jewelry design studio run by Jessie Alon, is a great example of going green. This studio's jewelry is made from recycled sterling silver, recycled glass, and reclaimed marble. The studio also recycles its stationery and cardboard.

How long before the market gets saturated with green products? Well-made, attractive jewelry will always sell. The "going green" aspect is the particular niche, and at present, it appears to have a long life.

There are many other jewelry making disciplines. Some jewelry artists make their jewelry from felt, feathers, and other types of fabric materials using a sewing machine as their jewelry making tool, while some use other nontraditional materials such as plastic and wood.

The Importance of Keeping a Design Sketchbook

While preparing for other work projects in the past, or perhaps while studying for tests, you have more than likely prepared an outline to organize your thoughts and make the task more manageable. A design sketchbook is the jewelry artist's outline.

Doodling in your design sketchbook encourages creative thinking. The more you doodle, the better you'll become at taking an abstract concept and turning it into a wearable design. I find that my doodling is a great source for future inspiration.

Use your sketchbook as a total brain dump. In the beginning, there are no good or bad ideas. What seems to be a bad design now could be the foundation of a great design in the future.

A sketchbook can be whatever size you like. Mine is a small notebook that fits in my purse (I carry a big purse). I particularly like notebooks that allow you to add and remove pages. This feature really comes in handy during the process of refining your design or deciding the design is a no-go.

Use your sketchbook to record line drawings of jewelry designs. Design ideas will come to you in the oddest places. The shape of a building or the curve of the road may be the inspiration for a pendant or necklace design. If your sketchbook is readily available, you can quickly draft a line drawing, make a few notes, and then refine the design later.

I also rip pictures out of magazines and tape them to pages in my sketchbook for future reference. I'm not just talking about other designers' work, but also color combinations or the arrangement of shapes in an advertisement—anything that will lend itself to a cool piece of jewelry in the future.

After a line drawing is complete, I annotate in my sketchbook the materials and techniques I believe will be suitable for this design. Using my sketchbook notes, I call up material prices from my database, double-check them with the current price of sterling silver or gold, and use this information to see if a design with an acceptable profit margin can be produced.

The sketchbook is also a great place to note the vendors from whom you will be purchasing the raw materials. In time, you'll have a solid relationship with a few pre-ferred vendors. However, occasionally you'll need a gemstone or a component that is sold by specialty vendors. It's nice to have this information included along with all of the other design details.

If the design passes the gross margin test, I construct a prototype using my sketchbook as a guide. While fabricating the prototype, I also make notes in my sketchbook detailing the step-by-step method used to make the piece of jewelry. This seems like a no-brainer, but it's easy to get excited about what you are making and forget to write down the actual process.

Even a day later, some aspects can become fuzzy. For example, did I use four inches of sterling silver wire or six to attach the clasp? You'll find that when making the prototype you'll use excess amounts of raw material as you refine the design. This is wasteful, and serves to reduce your profit margin if you continue to do so when you are in production mode.

Note in your sketchbook exactly how much of each component went into the design. In the example above, I may have cut six inches of sterling silver wire, but I only needed to use three inches. Keep track, as it adds up over time.

If your prototype didn't work out, it's back to the sketchbook to modify the design and make notes on any design alterations. This happens all the time. I'll think a

This page of the sketchbook shows a first draft of a pair of earrings with total view, ear-wire assembly, and detail of the bottom section of the drop. As the design is refined, I'll add expanded details to subsequent pages, with a photograph of the final completed version on the last page.

Victory Stone Earrings

2" diameter

18 gauge
SS Round wire

Ear wire formed
on tear drop
mandrel

dangle → crimp bead
18 gauge   1/2 round
          1/2 hard
SS wire

• gem stones - Fire mountain
   o chrysophase
   o white sapphire
   o emerald
• sterling silver wire -
          Rio grande

method will work and the piece ends up hanging funny or the materials just don't lend themselves to the technique.

Finally, once the design is a go, I take a picture of the finished product to add to the sketchbook. All of this may sound like a lot of work, but these steps work together to solidify the necessary underpinnings of your design process.

After the design is in production, I move all my notes and pictures related to the design out of the sketchbook and into a "finished goods" notebook. Specifications on how to make the piece and the exact components you use are invaluable resources when you hire others. It provides an exact road map on how to make the piece from start to finish, eliminating the need for in-depth training.

Now that you've had a chance to define your jewelry making business, your next step is to set up your home office and workshop.

3 Setting Up Your Office and Workshop

The good news about setting up a home-based business is that you most likely have many of the necessary office essentials already available in your home. Think about where you pay your bills or help your children with their homework. Can this area and furniture do double duty as your home office?

Office Essentials

Furniture and Office Equipment

Regardless of your business purpose, there are office essentials for every business. The basics include:

- Desk
- Comfortable chairs and floor mats
- File cabinets
- Sufficient lighting
- Postage meter and scale
- Calculator
- Photocopier
- Wastebasket
- Paper shredder
- Telephone
- Desktop organizers
- Computer carts and stands
- Cubicles and panels
- Fax
- Answering machine

- Postage and slide storage
- Surface protectors
- Foot/back rests
- Hooks, racks, and hangers
- Furniture castors
- Wire organizer systems

Determine which things you already have and which are necessary. For example, I've never had a postage meter. I have a small kitchen scale I use to calculate postage and I use self-adhesive postage stamps in the correct amount. However, I couldn't live without my shredder. It's not only an identify-theft issue but also one of destroying business-related proprietary documents.

Office-Supply Basics

Basic office supplies run the gamut from pens and pencils to scissors and manila file folders. Most households already have a certain amount of various office supplies. Three office supplies I cannot live without are sticky notes, white-out tape, and binder clips. I leave sticky notes all over the house as ideas occur to me. The white-out tape comes in handy for the sketchbook, and I prefer to clip rather than staple documents together.

Depending on the volume of your jewelry sales as a hobbyist, you might already have a receipt book. If not, this is an essential item if you plan to market your jewelry at craft shows or home parties—any place where it is awkward to set up a computer and printer to produce a customer receipt.

Even if you are wholesaling jewelry to retail shops, it might be easier for you to annotate the jewelry items on a handwritten receipt form. I've noticed that some smaller retail shops still use this method rather than a cash register.

If not using an accounting program to write checks, I also recommend getting three-to-the-page check forms. Although the binder the checks come in is bulky, this disadvantage is offset by the fact that you have big stubs on which you can diarize the complete check info. This comes in handy when preparing financial statements and at tax preparation time.

Another recommended business form is the proposal or quote form. This is a proposed sales agreement between your company and a customer. It contains contact information for the customer, and it lists the products and services you plan to provide to the customer. It also contains delivery and expiration dates, payment terms, and prices.

When might you use this type of form? Say a customer comes to you with a big job—maybe jewelry for the entire wedding party. You can use this form as your written formal document to detail all agreed-upon facts and circumstances. Always note if the customer deposit is nonrefundable. Make sure you completely describe the design, gemstones, and metals you will use in the design. While a sketch of the design is fine, a photograph of a prototype is much better. Of course, delivery date and price are two essentials.

Have the customer sign off on the proposal to protect yourself in case of dispute. There is no more fertile ground for disputes than that of wedding arrangements. After your customer approves your proposal, convert it to an invoice for billing purposes.

Using the Internet for Business Document Ideas

It's a good idea to troll around on the Internet looking for free examples of business and legal forms. That's how I got the lease for my rental home and a customer contract. Also, check out sites such as www.nolo.com. Look at their array of possible forms. You may see a form you didn't realize you needed that will come in handy.

Computer Equipment

Many households also already have a computer and various peripherals. Initially, buy only the essentials. Technology changes so rapidly. Adopt a wait-and-see attitude if a piece of computer gear is not presently 100 percent necessary.

Business Software Essentials

At a minimum, a business should have word processing and spreadsheet software. Optional but nice is an accounting package, at least for check writing.

Microsoft (Word and Excel) is the industry leader in this software field. I have computers with both the 2003 and 2007 applications. I prefer the 2003 version, as I

PROPOSAL

Maire Loughran Jewelry

Date: 10/28/20XX
Expiration Date:
11/15/20XX

TO

Lisa Baldwin
Baldwin Park Boutique
1150 Michigan Ave.
Chicago, IL 60656

Salesperson	Job	Delivery Date	Payment Terms
Maire	Baldwin Park	11/24/20XX	Upon Receipt

Description	Qty.	Unit Price	Discount	Line Total
Kits for Children's Jewelry Making Class	30	$10.00		$300.00
4-hour Instruction on 3rd Saturday in November	4	$50.00		$200.00
Christmas Necklaces – Various Gemstone Colors	10	$15.00		$150.00
Smith Job on Spec – Opal and Diamond Ring	1	$75.00		$75.00
2 Black Opals, approximately 43 carats	2	$500.00		$1,000.00
1 Emerald Cut Diamond, approximately 2 carats	1	$700.00		$700.00
Total Discount:			$0.00	
Subtotal:				$2,425.00
Sales Tax:				$0.00
Total:				$2,425.00

Proposal prepared by: Maire Loughran

This is a quotation on the goods named, subject to the conditions noted below: (Describe any conditions pertaining to these prices and any additional terms of the agreement. You may want to include contingencies that will affect the quotation.) To accept this quotation, sign here and return:

Thank you for your business!

Maire Loughran Jewelry

509 Lake Como Circle
Suite 12
Chicago, IL 60651

Phone: 321.555.1212 Fax: 321.555.2222 maire@maireloughranjewelry.com find it to be more user-friendly. If you are not a Microsoft fan, Corel markets a Word-Perfect office suite that includes word processing, spreadsheets, presentations, and e-mail applications.

If *free* is the price tag you are looking for, check out OpenOffice.org 3 software. It is a free downloadable office suite with a loyal client base dating back twenty years. It includes word processing, spreadsheets, databases, and much more. Find out more about this product at www.why.openoffice.org.

Other Free Software Options

Google Docs—Google provides free online document and spreadsheet programs. The cool thing about this is that you can access your files whenever you want from any computer that has Internet access (including iPhones). Find out more at docs .google.com.

Label Maker—Avery has a free label-maker program available for download at www.avery.com. Click Templates > Avery DesignPro. You can also import images to include on the labels. This program works on Avery labels.

Microsoft Office Templates—If you use various types of Microsoft products, there is a complete library of free downloadable templates. Check this out by going to www.office.microsoft.com. On the top toolbar click Templates.

Over the years, I've had a chance to use many different types of boxed accounting software. In the under-$200 price range there is little difference between the various products. If you are a die-hard Microsoft fan, I recommend a new player in the boxed accounting software field—Microsoft Office Accounting Professional 2009.

What truly sets this program apart is the awesome way it interfaces with eBay, PayPal, and Microsoft's other programs, like Word and Excel. Because Accounting 2009's invoices are compatible with Word, you can print them with your company logo. The program can also integrate your contact information from Outlook. This will save you both time and money.

Jewelry Making Software Suggestions

There are some very cool software applications to help you accurately cost and price your jewelry line. A single piece of jewelry can use an unlimited amount of gemstones, findings, and components. Findings are those small but necessary jewelry making items such as crimp beads and head pins. The term component refers to jewelry making gemstones and metals. You can ballpark the cost of raw materials when setting your price. However, it is more cost-effective and efficient to use a software program that tracks raw material costs and also prices the product using your desired markup.

Jewelry Designer MANAGER

One program I highly recommend is Rio Grande's Jewelry Designer MANAGER software. For a home-based business, the basic version—priced at under $100—is powerful enough. In addition to the markup feature, it also tracks inventory and vendors, so when you run out of a clasp you won't have to riffle through old invoices to figure out which vendor carries it.

Rio Grande sells online to the jewelry making public, but you must set up an account before you can access their catalog and make a purchase.

Rhino

The serious jewelry designer specializing in custom design work will find Rhino software a fantastic tool to create 3-D design models to show a client before starting work on the project. The software allows you to keep a virtual inventory of jewelry. You imagine the design and use the software to create an image that looks exactly like a real piece of jewelry.

Of course, the catch here is that you need the jewelry making skills to fabricate the actual jewelry for sale. Pricey at just under $1,000, Rhino provides an evaluation download that works twenty-five times so you can try before you buy.

Digital Photography Software

Digital photography and image-editing software is necessary for a jewelry making business. I can't tell you the number of times I've shot a piece of jewelry and it's looked fantastic. Fantastic, until I noticed that speck of dust on the backdrop that only showed up in the macro version of the shot. Using editing software, one click of the mouse and the speck is gone without having to reshoot the jewelry.

The most common commercial application of this software is removal of red-eye in portraits. Think of this software for your jewelry images in the same way. Weird glare? Tone it down. Not happy with the backdrop? Brighten it up or make it completely white.

Adobe Photoshop

There are many different editing software packages. Adobe Photoshop is very popular and is the benchmark by which other editing software programs are judged. Whatever you want to do with your image is probably possible with Photoshop. For example, you can use it to adjust exposures or color balance and to resize your image.

A less-complicated version of Photoshop, Adobe Photoshop Elements performs all basic editing tasks and offers step-by-step editing assistance. It also shows you how to organize and share your images in Web galleries.

Adobe has an online application called Photoshop Express that is worth a look. Express covers all the bases for digital images: organizing, editing, and sharing. It also interfaces with other services like Facebook, Photobucket, and Picasa. Find it by doing a Google search for "photoshop express."

GIMP

If free is your cup of tea, check out the GNU Image Manipulation Program (GIMP). GIMP is a freely distributed piece of software and duplicates many of the tasks available in Photoshop, such as photo retouching and image composition. If you have used Photoshop in the past, you'll find GIMP operates in a similar fashion. Find out more about GIMP by Googling the keyword "gimp."

Office Telephone and Fax

It's not necessary for a home-based business to have a business line. The telephone company's monthly charge for a business line is much more than a personal line. Why waste the money when having two personal lines, one earmarked for business, will serve the same purpose.

Most homes built from the 1970s on are already wired for two lines. If you live in an older home, perhaps a prior owner had the home rewired. I lived in a 1920s arts and crafts bungalow whose prior owner (to my relief) had already installed two lines.

You might have two lines and not know it if the jack is not properly wired. It is a simple task to connect the appropriate wires. I've done it many times and I'm not an electrical wizard. Instructions are online at many home improvement sites. Don't want to mess around with wires? Call your local telephone company to have a tech wire your jack.

Telephone Income Tax Deduction

The IRS allows a full deduction for the second line regardless of whether the phone company views it as a business or a personal line.

However, to take any write-off for your landline phone, you must have two separate lines. If you only have one, you are not allowed to write off half the cost.

Regardless of whether you have one or two telephone lines, you can write off the cost of any long-distance business-related telephone calls.

From the number of people I see in public gabbing on cell phones, I have to assume that just about everyone has one. Is it feasible to use that type of service for your business line? If you get good reception generally, dropped calls are few, and it doesn't sound like you're in a wind tunnel, then a cell phone is perfectly fine to use for your business.

Should you want to create the illusion that you are running more than a one-person shop, consider the use of an auto attendant. It will answer your phone with your company's menu and transfer callers to the correct person or department. Maybe you're the only correct person for all departments, but your caller doesn't have to know that.

Most auto attendants will transfer the call to your cell or any other phone if you don't pick up. Some maintain a phone line for you and transfer calls to any other telephone number you wish. This eliminates the need to wire your home for two lines.

It's been years since I've had a dedicated fax line. I prefer to use one of the online fax services that send incoming faxes to you via e-mail. I travel a lot. No matter where I am, I always have access to faxes from customers.

Most give you the option of having the fax number set up with your local area code or with an 800 number. You generally won't need to spend the additional money for an 800 number. The setup is extremely professional: The fax line rings once and your sender is connected. Gone is the fax line ringing at your home in the middle of the night with junk faxes. In addition, there is nothing more vexing for your customer than to tell them to call back so you can turn the fax on.

Some also handle outgoing faxes through the Internet as well. I prefer the old-fashioned way of sending faxes via the telephone line. Fax machines are cheap. I have one connected to a spare jack with the ringer turned off. Many documents I have to fax are not computer-generated. Having a fax machine eliminates the need to scan documents into the computer prior to faxing.

Find auto attendants and eFax services by doing a Google search using those key phrases.

Set Up a Shipping Account

There are three primary players in the shipping business: United Parcel Service (UPS), Federal Express (FedEx), and the United States Postal Service (USPS).

Rather than stand in line at the post office to mail packages, you can use USPS's Click-N-Ship® service. It's quick, easy, and reliable. You will need to set up an account online at www.usps.com that captures your address and payment information. When you're ready to ship, log into your account, fill in the recipient's address information, package weight, and desired delivery speed. Print the mailing label and you're done!

As far as getting the package into the actual mail system, there is a sixteen-ounce weight limit for items dropped into a mailbox. If your package weighs less than that and it fits through the slot, drop it into a regular mailbox.

Otherwise, you have to go into the post office. Many postal employees don't have a problem with you leaving Click-N-Ship® packages to be mailed at the end of the counter. If you're not sure, stand in line the first time you mail a package and ask. You can also request free carrier pickup. When your carrier drops off your mail, they pick up any outgoing packages.

The USPS doesn't pick up at all residential addresses. While on the Web site, arranging to ship your package, you can enter your zip code to confirm that this service is available to you.

If you need to ship a bulky package or require insurance, I recommend using a carrier such as UPS or FedEx. Both allow you to set up an account and make shipping arrangements online. Residential pickup is a service of both as well, for an additional fee.

I use both and find there is little difference between the two in service. Cost of shipping is a primary concern, and there can be differences in price between UPS and FedEx. Until you are familiar with the pricing, check both to see which is less expensive.

To keep from having to pay the additional pickup charge, you might want to use the vendor that has a drop-off location most convenient to your residence.

Workshop Essentials

Workbench

The most important piece of equipment for a jewelry maker is a solid (preferably wooden) workbench. To make your work space more ergonomic, it should hit you at about mid-chest level. You do not have to buy a fancy workbench. Any plain table will do, although a professional workbench is set up with handy drawers, dividers, and railings to keep jewelry components from dropping on the floor.

If you opt to use a plain wooden table and it's too low, you can raise it up on sturdy blocks of wood glued or screwed to the bottom of the legs. It's best to have a wooden workbench because you'll be bolting, nailing, and drilling holes into it to attach other jewelry making tools and devices. I have a few jigs nailed into my workbench because it is easier to work with them. Metal tables don't provide the same flexible surface.

Flex Shaft

You should also own a flex shaft as it reduces the amount of time it takes to make a piece of jewelry and improve its appearance. This tool is similar to the Dremel tools you may be using to sand, shape, polish, and diamond-set, but it's more powerful. For example, it works at variable speeds, many of which are higher than Dremel tools, so that the task at hand can be accomplished more quickly.

Work Lights and Magnifiers

Proper work lights and magnifiers are a jewelry making essential. I feel that natural light is best when working on your craft. However, there will be days that are overcast or times when you will be working at night. In addition, if your workshop is in a basement or garage without natural lighting, you have no alternative.

Try to use bright lights with bulbs that simulate natural daylight. You'll have less eyestrain, and the colors used in your designs will be true. Lacking that, any lights that are bright and steady will do.

Unless you're Superman, you'll occasionally be using a magnifier. They come in many forms. Some are bolted to your workbench and have a flexible neck for adjustment. You can also buy a pair of jeweler's goggles with interchangeable lenses in different magnification powers.

I use both goggles and a large round magnifier on a rolling stand that also has a light source. The round magnifier is similar in appearance to the magnifier your dentist uses. Magnifying goggles when combined with daylight are sufficient for most jewelry making purposes.

Photographic Equipment

If you plan to hire a photographer, you won't have a great need for photographic equipment. However, professional jewelry photographers are very expensive. Moreover, unless you are lucky enough to have a good one within driving distance, you will have the extra expense of insuring and shipping your jewelry back and forth for the photo shoot.

Photographic equipment has really dropped in price over the last decade. The up-front cost is still somewhat pricey, but you'll break even after the cost of just one professional photo shoot. Keep in mind these two terms when purchasing a digital camera:

- 72 pixels per inch (ppi): Geared toward viewing images on a computer monitor
- 300 ppi: Appropriate for publishing and software publishing

While you're at the camera store, purchase a tripod. A tripod has a screw-on base to place the camera. This stabilizes the camera, eliminating the dreaded blurry-picture camera shake. A bonus: Tripods are inexpensive and will last for years.

Two other mandatory items of photographic equipment are light diffusers and backdrops. Over the years, I've read articles where jewelry makers describe how they go out into their backyard on a sunny day and shoot their jewelry under a tent made from a white sheet. Some also place their jewelry in a clear plastic tub, which acts as the light diffuser. Examples of these photos accompany the articles, and honestly, they are second-rate.

Goodness—do you want to leave your customers with the image of you standing outside with a sheet over your head while photographing your jewelry? There are professional alternatives at a moderate cost.

When I started out, I did waste a lot of time shooting and reshooting jewelry using natural sunlight until it looked just right. Even then, the results were less than stellar. After researching alternatives, I purchased an EZcube light box© from the Table Top Studio-Store. I highly recommend this light diffuser. The Jewelry Photo Kit comes with a small and large tent, three light sources, platforms, and more.

Using a professional light diffuser such as the EZcube allows you to soften shadows, reduce glare, increase gemstone brilliance, and create a clean, uncluttered background for your image. Priced at under $300, it is well worth the cash outlay.

Digital Camera Basics

Brand doesn't matter as much as camera features.

A simple point-and-shoot camera with at least 3.2 megapixels, 5 cm (2 inch) macros, and 10X zoom will do the job if all you want to do is upload images to the Internet. Not sure what this means? Here's a quick tutorial:

Digital cameras capture images as pixel elements; a megapixel is equal to a million pixels. The more pixels, the higher the image resolution. However, this is only one benchmark in the suitability of a digital camera for shooting jewelry.

A macro setting changes the focus of the camera so it can focus on very close objects.

Zooming and focusing work hand in hand. When a camera "zooms," it moves in closer to the object being photographed. Just because the camera can zoom in doesn't mean it can focus on the object.

If you need a digital camera to also take pictures at 300 ppi for print ads and submission to magazines or juried shows, consider the extra expense of buying a camera with a digital single lens reflex (DSLR).

When selecting a digital camera, make a personal visit to a camera store and take a piece of jewelry with you. Take shots with a few cameras in your price range and ask the clerk to download the images onto a computer so you can see how they render. Evaluate the images and purchase the best you can in your price range.

I now use an Ortery Photosimile Light Box. It's quite a bit pricier than the EZcube at just over $1,000, but the volume of jewelry photography I do has justified the additional expense. It's a square, lightweight box with built-in adjustable lighting.

The software for the light box allows my computer and camera to talk to each other, which speeds up the photography process.

Regardless of which light diffuser method you prefer, I feel that you obtain a more professional image by using backdrops. This is a matter of personal preference. Look at some online jewelry outlets and catalogs. Most will show the jewelry with a dead white background. This effect is achieved either through use of your camera's settings and a good diffuser (Table Top Studios devotes six pages to this topic in their how-to's) or by Photoshopping the image.

Now take a look at jewelry images shown in jewelry art books or high-fashion jewelry designers' Web sites. Most of these images are shot on a gradient backdrop. By *gradient*, I mean the color is darker at the top and gradually lightens toward the bottom.

Use Photoshop or a similar program to achieve this effect. You can use Photoshop's gradient tool and a color printer to print a gradient sheet, or just tell the software to place your image on a gradient background. Some photographic supply shops sell gradient paper. However, it is difficult to find paper scaled down to the size needed to shoot jewelry.

You can also make your own gradient paper. Get a piece of glossy or semi-glossy paper in the correct size. Spray-paint one end with flat paint in one color. Spray-paint the other end with flat paint in the second color. Where the overlap occurs, move the cans out further to mist the overlap to get an intermediate color. This creates the same effect used by portrait photographers, but on a smaller scale.

Free Digital Jewelry Photography Tips

Whether or not you buy an EZcube, the Table Top Studio-Store has pages of fantastic jewelry photography tips accessible via the Internet. For example, you can find out how to underlight translucent beads or prop up focal beads with wax. In addition, detailed instructions explain how to photograph pearls so they appear rounder, with the proper amount of dimension, or how to suspend earrings. Find the index by doing a Google search using the key phrase "ezcube how-to."

Safety Equipment

This list is not all-inclusive. Many of the chemicals and procedures used to make jewelry can be dangerous. If you have any questions at all about the safety of your work space, consult your safety supply company's representative.

It is important to take steps to protect your eyes, lungs, and hands during the jewelry making process. Some jewelry making procedures throw off chemical odors and dust. There is also the risk that a stray bit of metal will pop up and hit you in the face or eye.

Luckily, all these risks are easy to manage if you wear the correct protective gear. Always wear a pair of safety goggles when working. Even a smooth, round gemstone bead popping up from its setting can do significant damage if it hits you square in the eye.

Use the proper tongs when placing or removing metal components from caustic chemicals during the fabrication process. For example, copper tongs keep your fingers out of pickle and don't contaminate the pickling solution.

Make sure you use a good pick with a stay-cool handle if manipulating jewelry pieces while soldering. I recommend leather finger guards for those who polish or grind their jewelry. In addition, use heat blocks as a soldering base to avoid starting a fire in your workshop.

Finally, be certain to protect your lungs. It's important you keep from inhaling the particle by-product of jewelry making, and you want to avoid breathing in vapors that over time can be quite damaging to your lungs. You can use a 3M particle respirator mask for the dust kicked off when you are grinding, sanding, polishing, or sweeping up your work space. It's similar in appearance to a doctor's mask and is very lightweight and comfortable to wear.

Make sure that the National Institute for Occupational Safety and Health (NIOSH) approves any mask you buy. NIOSH is part of the U.S. Department of Health and Human Services. Its mission is to prevent workplace illnesses and injury.

I developed asthma a few years back while renovating a cottage that had a hidden mold problem. Therefore, I wear a full-out faceplate with interchangeable cartridges for dust and organic vapors. The faceplate I use is manufactured by 3M. While not quite as comfortable as a mask, it provides more protection. I highly recommend the use of this sort of product rather than relying on a mask.

Capture Precious Metal for Scrap

It's the nature of the beast that as you create jewelry, there will be metal scraps. Whether you're using sterling silver or karated gold, it's a total waste of your money if you do not recycle these scraps. Some jewelry artists melt the scraps down to use again or incorporate them into an abstract piece of jewelry.

If that's too much work, many jewelry supply companies will purchase your sterling silver and karated gold scraps to recycle. If you purchase a professional jeweler's workbench, they are normally outfitted with a catch tray to store your scraps. Otherwise, just carefully sweep up the dust and metal bits and pieces and store the sterling silver or karated gold separately until you have enough to sell.

You may have a local jewelry supplier that buys back scraps. Otherwise, many online suppliers will do so. Prices paid will vary, so check with the company for an exact quote. Online vendor Rio Grande buys scraps. The price they pay fluctuates based on the market. Visit their Web site for more information on how to prepare your scraps for recycling.

Transforming the Personal Workshop into a Production Workshop

You've probably allocated a corner of your home for making your jewelry. Well, you're in business now. It's time to take your work area a bit more seriously.

Flooring

The first thing I recommend if you have your workshop in a spare room with carpeted floors is to pull the carpeting up from the tack bars and roll it clear from the work area. You'll be down to the subfloor, which is either concrete or board. It's easier to keep either of these clean than it is carpeting. Of course, watch out for the tack bars, as they are painful if you step on them. If you're a beader who does no fabrication of metal components that causes dust, then carpeting is A-OK.

If you work with beads or gemstones that can crack if dropped, keep a mat under the area where you work with these materials. A mat also captures any spare bead or part that jumps off your workbench. If you're a beader, you know there is nothing more aggravating than searching for a small mm bead. I've found that mats made of the same type of material as yoga mats both protect and capture gemstones. However, this type of mat is not appropriate for use anywhere you solder or use caustic chemicals.

Storage

It's important to have an organized storage system for both jewelry making components and tools. Just the other day, I was searching for some teardrop-shaped green gemstones that I know I have in stock. I couldn't find those but I did find some expensive emerald 3mm x 5mm faceted gemstones that I had completely forgotten about.

Not having an organized storage system will cost you the time spent searching, as well as money if you have to reorder components you know you own but cannot find. Set your storage system up in whatever way makes the most sense to you. I keep my gemstones organized by color, then subcategorized by size. I store those I use most frequently, such as aquamarine, emerald, and opal, in their own drawer.

The same is true with my metal components. Sterling silver, gold-filled, and karated gold are stored with like metals, further organized by type. For example, all sterling-silver crimp beads, fancy bails, etc., are stored together.

Have a similar storage system for your tools. I hang my basic jewelry making tools on hooks and keep the smaller tools such as files in a labeled drawer.

Ventilation

Ideally, if one is soldering, working with chemicals, or grinding, local ventilation should be put in place. This means that you place a sucking device very close to the work area that is generating the dust, mist, or fumes, so you can suck them away as you produce them. You should vent the device outside.

This can be difficult to arrange in a home work space. There are small workshop fans (sold in jewelry-makers' catalogs) that can be placed at the immediate work location. Typically, they are positioned so they suck the air *away* from the work area and out through an open window. Of course, this only works if you are located next to an open window. Cross ventilation is an alternative, but is not as effective. As I said in the beginning of this section, if you are unsure about the safety of your ventilation system, ask an expert.

Hazardous Storage

All hazardous material purchased from a jewelry supply house will come with a Material Safety Data Sheet (MSDS). This sheet has full details about the potential side effects of improper use of the product, and describes first-aid or emergency procedures. It also gives guidelines on storage and cleanup.

Obviously, all jewelry making supplies and tools have the potential to harm. This runs the gamut from a child choking on a small bead to cutting himself on a saw or pick. Follow the exact directions on the MSDS. If the product did not come with an MSDS, these same cautions are usually printed on the product label.

If you have young children, do not take chances. Secure all your jewelry supplies and tools in an inaccessible location. Keep hazardous materials under lock and key. Whether or not there are young children in your home, store chemicals and the like at the proper temperature in clearly labeled containers.

The first three chapters of this book have given you the chance to consider the basics and organize your business ideas. Now it's time to firm up your estimations by writing your business plan.

4 The Business Plan: Your Plan of Action

I could probably get from Chicago, Illinois, to St. Louis, Missouri, without a road map if I had to. However, having a plan of action as to which highways to take makes the trip more efficient. The same holds true for your business when you draft and update a business plan.

A business plan is your road map to success for your business. When you research and thoroughly organize your plan of attack, from setting prices to personnel policies, the chances of having your business succeed increase substantially. Additionally, a business plan saves money. After researching your competition, vendors, and current industry events, you may find that your original direction isn't feasible.

If that's the case, what have you lost? Certainly, you've lost some research time, but you've gained perspective, and you've definitely not lost the cash you would have spent for the start-up with your original vision. Suppose you'd decided to quit your day job? That would have been a disaster.

All lending institutions will ask for your business plan as part of your loan package. Maybe you are funding the start-up by taking a second mortgage on your home. You might shrug your shoulders and feel writing the plan is too much work—why bother if equity in the home is the source of your cash? I consider a proper business plan even more important in these circumstances. Just as quitting the job that is your primary source of income without a proper plan, placing the roof over your head in jeopardy is just as foolhardy.

Business plans come in handy for setting long- and short-term goals. Honestly, a brand-new business's short-term goal is to break even. However, what comes after that? Do you want to build the business into a full-time enterprise and quit your day job? Maybe you want to make enough money on the side to take a fantastic vacation each year, or to pay for your children's higher education with ease.

Everyone has different goals, and these different goals dictate different action plans and commitment levels. A well-thought-out business plan moves you from inception to actualization with confidence.

Remember, a business plan is a fluid document. Update your business plan as your business grows or changes direction.

Get Free Business Plan Help

The Small Business Administration (SBA) has extremely helpful resources to help you write your business plan. Go to www.sba.gov and select the Small Business Planner link on the top navigation bar. There you'll find fantastic information on how to write a business plan, along with many other aspects of running a small business.

Looking for a mentor? The Service Corps of Retired Executives (SCORE) provides online and in-person mentoring. Find out more at www.score.org. Services at both the SBA and SCORE are free.

Entrepreneur.com also gives some business plan advice and has a handy state-by-state listing of commerce department resources for additional help. You can access this page by doing a Google search using the key phrase "entrepreneur connect get help with your business plan."

Elements of a Business Plan

Writing a business plan is both tedious and exhilarating. It's tedious as you work through each section, dealing with problems and exploring alternative solutions. It's exhilarating as you find out that yes, this is a doable proposition.

In this chapter, I have laid out all the elements of a proper business plan. Remember, though, that every business is different, and the steps to success are unique. Therefore, your business plan should also be unique. As you'll notice as I walk you through each section, not every section requires a long, drawn-out explanation. With the business plan, like most things in life, less is more. You're not paid by the word, so don't gunk it up with unnecessary rhetoric.

There are seven main sections in a business plan. Many business plans also include a conclusion, appendix, or exit strategy. There is no single right or wrong way to develop a business plan. However, some elements are common to all well-written plans. Stick to this basic business plan road map and you'll cover all the common elements during your drive from point A to point B. Incorporate your long- and short-term goals as part of these sections.

Executive Summary

Consider the purpose of the business and briefly state how you intend to achieve that purpose. The objective here is to be concise and to the point, with further elaboration to come in the following sections.

Basic Company Information

List the contact information for your business here: name, address, phone and fax number(s), how long you have been in business, hours of operation—you get the idea. As your business grows, you may add more locations in different cities; this would be the section to address that fact.

Products or Services Offered

Give this serious thought as you describe the goods and services your company intends to provide. Elaborate on your mode of delivery in the Plan of Operations section.

For example, you make gorgeous gemstone necklaces and bracelets. Give a detailed description of the gemstones, components, and techniques you use in this section. The Plan of Operations section will discuss whether you plan to string the gemstone beads yourself, outsource the procedure, or hire employees to do it in-house.

Facts about Your Industry, Competition, and Market

Discuss the jewelry making industry, particularly the niche in which you plan to place yourself. Discuss your competition and your customers, especially how you plan to beat the competition.

I suggest that you do a lot of research on various well-known jewelry designers, focusing on how they got their start in the business. It's amazing how many famous designers fell into the business while pursuing other careers. Helpful as well is to see how successful designers start with a basic idea or skill and then build it into a multimillion-dollar brand name.

Use the careers of successful jewelry designers to both inspire you and help you fill in the missing pieces of your road map to success. Certainly, being successful in any business takes a certain amount of luck and grit. However, if I've learned anything in my years of self-employment, it's that many times we make our own luck.

Recommended Reading

One book that I highly recommend is *Robert Lee Morris: The Power of Jewelry.* Written by Morris, with a foreword by Donna Karan, it offers a fascinating look at Morris's creative process and career. More important, it details not only his numerous successes but also his defeats, such as proudly showing a piece to a gallery owner and being told that perhaps he should pursue another career, like driving a truck, or the law. This brutal critique of his work caused him to take a step back and evaluate what he was attempting to create.

Management, Organization, and Ownership

If this business is your baby and you're handling all management aspects yourself, this section is brief. Ownership refers to choice of business entity and is a decision that you must make now.

Selection of Business Entity

Your next step is selection of business entity. You cannot open a business bank account or apply for a business license without having made this selection. Consider this carefully, as this decision will affect the financial and management aspects of how you do business.

Sole Proprietorship

The sole proprietorship is the easiest type of business entity to start up, and the least expensive to maintain. Once you make your first sale or incur your first business expense, you are officially in business. There are no expensive filings as is the case with a corporation or flow-through. The sole proprietor reports the net income of the business as part of the 1040 form, so you reduce tax-preparation hassle and expense as well.

A sole proprietorship has one and only one owner—hence, the word *sole*. It cannot be owned by a husband and wife, brother and sister, or group of friends. However, the sole proprietorship can have as many employees as it likes or needs.

Unless the sole proprietorship has employees, this type of business entity is unique in that it can operate under the owner's Social Security number. You must obtain a Federal Employer Identification Number (FEIN) if you hire employees. Will you have legitimate contractors? You can also use your Social Security number to issue 1099Ms.

The sole proprietor is not an employee of the business, so you will not receive a paycheck. A sole proprietor receives a draw check. You don't withhold employment taxes from the draw check. You want to be paid $500? Write yourself a check for $500—it's that easy.

Of course, you will eventually have to pay taxes. You pay self-employment tax and income tax on the sole proprietorship net income, with estimated tax deposits periodically through the year, or on your 1040 form when filed.

The major disadvantage to being a sole proprietorship is the liability issue. A sole proprietor without exception is responsible for all debts and actions taken against the business. However, unless you are selling an edible or potentially dangerous product, the chance that one of your customers will sue you is probably remote. To cover that eventuality, I recommend that all businesses, not just sole proprietorships, acquire business liability insurance.

Due to the ease of setup and operation, many consulting and design small business owners start out as sole proprietors and never feel the need to convert the business to another type of entity.

Corporation

Unlike the sole proprietorship, a corporation is a separate and distinct legal entity. The big selling point for incorporation is the limited liability aspect. With very few exceptions, you as the shareholder or officer of the corporation are not personally responsible for any actions taken against the business.

You stake ownership rights to the corporation by purchasing shares of its stock. The number of shares of stock sold determines ownership percentage. If you purchase the only share of stock issued, you are the 100 percent shareholder, totally in control of the corporation and all decision making.

It is more complicated to set up a corporation, as you have legal filing requirements with both your state and the federal government. All corporations have to apply for a FEIN from the Internal Revenue Service. Paying yourself becomes more involved because you receive an employee paycheck rather than receiving a straight-up draw check like a sole proprietor.

Tax-return preparation for a corporation is more expensive. A corporation files a federal Form 1120, which requires keeping both balance sheet and income statement figures. A sole proprietorship is only required to report income statement figures. In addition, you also have the responsibility of preparing quarterly payroll tax returns to report wages paid, even if you are the only employee. Most states also require that you file returns and pay tax on corporate net income as well.

Flow-Through

Back in the day, the only flow-through type of entity was a partnership. Currently, business owners have a choice between partnerships, S Corporations, Limited Liability Companies, and more.

Brief Comparison of the Three Types of Entities

Type	Management	Liability	Taxation
Sole Proprietorship	Self Directed	Unlimited	At owner's individual tax rate
Corporation	Centralized	Limited	Profit taxed at corporate rate
Flow-Through	All three aspects will vary based upon type of flow-through entity selected		

No matter what the structure or name, with a flow-through entity, net income or loss *flows through* the business and is taxed on your 1040. What's the advantage of being a flow-through? With this setup, the business is combining aspects of a sole proprietorship with the limited liability aspects of a corporation.

Flow-through entities can have complicated rules. For example, if you are the general partner in a partnership, you lose the limited liability protection. Always consult a professional when considering the selection of a flow-through entity.

While taxable income flows through to your personal 1040, all flow-through entities are required to file a federal informational tax return. Some states also have the same requirement. Depending on which flow-through entity you select, you might receive a draw or you might receive a paycheck.

Marketing Plan

I fully explore different suggestions on how to market a jewelry making business in the marketing chapter of this book (see chapter 10). If you've done your research, you should have some basic ideas of your own. Jot down bullet points and flesh out exactly how you plan to market your business.

Remember, the business plan is not set in stone. If you feel your first marketing plan is just not getting the job done, or the cost-benefit analysis doesn't pan out, revise, revise, revise. Update your business plan with these revisions.

Plan of Operations

This is your A to Z on the running of your business. Since it's a home-based business, you won't have an exhaustive listing of employees or store hours of operation. You do need to address other aspects of running the business, however.

I find that it's helpful to think about what you feel makes up a typical day in the life of a jewelry designer. Based upon my experience, here are some basic operational tasks in the jewelry making business:

- Keep track of various shows, contests, juried competitions, and track the status of your applications.
- Research and maintain a potential customer contact list. Contact at least one new potential customer from this list each day. Update your calendar with a follow-up date.
- Keep track of various trade shows that are within a feasible traveling dis-

tance from your home. Networking is a great way to make vendor contacts and to obtain possible leads on customers.

- Detail how you plan to comply with all local, state, and federal regulations.
- Decide on a shipping schedule. It's not time-efficient for a home-based business to ship customer orders every day. Mondays and Thursdays work well for me.
- Decide on how you will manage your inventory. Are you going to adopt a just-in-time system, where you only order new supplies when you are almost out? Maybe you want to have a stock of basic supplies always on hand.
- How about research into new products, procedures, and scheduling time for continuing education? What about streamlining your jewelry fabrication so that you can go about it in an assembly-line fashion? Alternatively, do you prefer starting and completely finishing a piece before you move on to your next design?
- Vendor wholesale analysis is also very important to discuss. What's your plan to maximum volume purchasing without tying up too much cash in inventory?

Financial Assumptions and Projections

Unless you have signed contracts from customers, projecting gross receipts is guesswork at best. That's why it's crucial to take the prior sections of the business plan seriously. You use all the research and knowledge you gain by working through the business plan and calculate the unknowns in your financial statements with an educated guess.

Expenses are easier to project. There are common start-up and operating expenses for all businesses. Based upon your chosen field of jewelry design, there are also unique expenses. Look back to chapter 2 of this book to refresh your memory on start-up expenses if need be.

Make sure you also include a section that explains your sources of cash. This consists of savings, borrowing, and putting to use items you already own. If you use your personal computer, desk, chair, and digital camera for your business, that is an investment by you, the owner, just the same as any cash you've loaned to the business for start-up.

Include an Income Statement, Balance Sheet, Statement of Cash Flows, and Break-Even Point Analysis. An Income Statement shows business revenue and expenses. Assets, liabilities, and owner's equity go on the balance sheet. Look to chapter 6 for examples of these three statements and more information about how you prepare them.

Break-even point analysis is a very important tool when preparing a business plan. It's used to figure out the volume of sales needed to cover both your *variable* and *fixed* costs. If your analysis shows you that an unlikely volume of jewelry sales is needed for you to break even, then it's back to the drawing board as you find ways to reduce expenses, increase per-unit revenue, or both. More info about break-even point analysis is contained in chapter 6.

Quick Guide to Variable Versus Fixed Expenses

Variable expenses are those that fluctuate based on the number of units sold. For example, if you make and sell five necklaces, your variable expense reflects the materials cost for those five necklaces only.

Fixed expenses do not change based upon your jewelry sales. A very good example of a fixed expense is your telephone bill. If you have a business line that costs $75 per month, no matter if you sell one piece of jewelry or a million, you still have the same $75 telephone bill each month.

While it's easy to understand the basic concept of what goes into a business plan, sometimes it's hard to get your ideas organized. To help you, I have prepared a simple business plan for my fictitious period jewelry company:

Business Plan for Maire Loughran Jewelry Designs

Contact Information:

PO XXXX

Chicago, IL 60626

773.555.1212

maire@maireloughran.com

This document contains confidential information. It is disclosed to you for informational purposes only. Its contents shall remain the property of Maire Loughran Jewelry Designs and shall be returned to Maire Loughran Jewelry Designs when requested. Note: This is a business plan and does not imply an offering of securities.

Table of Contents

Executive Summary

Maire Loughran Jewelry Designs (MJD) specializes in period jewelry re-created as costume jewelry. Jewelry from the past has always been of interest to a certain class of jewelry buyers. We intend to fulfill that need by researching authentic historical designs and then fabricating them as costume jewelry.

Using plated metals instead of precious, and crystals in place of actual gemstones, will allow us to keep our retail price point below $50. This will increase our appeal across all age ranges, and especially in our target market of females under the age of thirty.

Company Information

MJD is a sole proprietorship. The business began in 2007. Its original purpose was to provide mid-range bridge jewelry targeting those interested in buying jewelry with a purpose—specifically, ritual or ethnic jewelry.

In ancient ethnic jewelry, the elements of the gemstones and precious metals were carefully combined to bring about the desired effect. For example, green gemstones, particularly the beautiful and precious emerald, were used therapeutically to relieve eyestrain.

After much consideration, it was the decision of the Company that the target market for this type of jewelry is much too narrow and has been filled by established vendors with ties to various communities. However, the Company is moving forward by applying this same research methodology in the design of period jewelry.

Maire Loughran is the sole proprietor. She brings five years of jewelry making experience to the business. She has a degree in art history from Loyola University, Chicago, Illinois, and has attended numerous classes in jewelry making and design at the Arrowmont School of Arts and Crafts in Gatlinburg, Tennessee.

Products or Services Offered

There are no completely new ideas in fashion or jewelry. For example, jewelry design star David Yurman's signature style, the original twisted-cable design, is similar to that of the ancient Celtic torc. When asked, most fashion designers will reference historical influences as the base of their design line (i.e., a flowing dress arranged toga-style).

We plan to capitalize on this fact by re-creating jewelry from the past. Our model begins with inspiration from jewelry worn by Elizabeth I of England, known as the costume jewelry queen, and our line is carried forward to the 1920s. Initially, we do not plan to use Ancient Egypt as a possible design line, as we feel this market is saturated.

Looking at many contemporaneous design lines, it is evident they are pulling the inspiration for their designs from the past. However, we plan to capitalize on the fact that our jewelry is inspired by historical figures such as Marie Antoinette. This includes aggressively marketing the jewelry as period jewelry, and providing the customer with a brief history of the design.

Whenever the economic picture seems a bit uncertain, most customers scale back on discretionary items and are reluctant to take on any additional financial obligations. Jewelry is often classified as a discretionary item.

As a rule, the more wealth one has accumulated, the less one will be impacted by the ebb and flow of economic conditions. There will always be a market for the extremely expensive designer jewelry one sees in chichi magazines. Along the same lines, costume jewelry in the under-$50 range will probably see little trickle-down effect in a poor economy.

Using plated metals and crystals or glass with this model, it is possible to keep this jewelry line in the realm of mid-level costume jewelry, thus providing the Company with the ability to weather most economic storms. Costume jewelry in the under-$50 price range has consistently been a good performer in times of all economic circumstances.

We will initially use plated metal components that are ready-made. Eventually, we plan to custom-design our own jewelry components and have them cast to our specifications.

MJD will cover all design bases by producing scaled-down lines suitable for the office and more elaborate lines for evening wear.

Industry, Competition, and Market

The *U.S. Bureau of Labor Occupational Outlook Handbook* for 2008–2009 rates employment prospects for jewelers as favorable. Favorable employment conditions indicate a continuing demand for jewelry.

Demographically, our target market will be females under thirty. Buying patterns show that more than half of new charm bracelet purchases are made by females under thirty. Many equate a charm bracelet to a wearable piece of history.

Additionally, that age range is fascinated by tragic or heroic historical figures. Our period pieces of jewelry tie together both of these elements.

There is no direct competition in the under-$50 period jewelry industry. Well-known costume jewelers such as Monet and Trifari are in abundant supply; however, none of them specialize in period jewelry. While many famous designers such as Vera Wang and Subversive are moving into the costume jewelry arena, they are not marketing period designs.

The Company doesn't feel it is limiting itself by producing period jewelry. The jewelry is attractive, wearable, and priced correctly. The hook or niche is the fact that its design style is that of period jewelry.

Management, Organization, and Ownership

MJD is a sole proprietorship organized and managed by Maire Loughran. Initially all design, fabrication, and marketing efforts are the responsibility of Ms. Loughran. As the Company grows, these positions will be filled, part- or full-time, as needed.

Marketing Plan

[Note: I discuss the topic of marketing your jewelry in chapter 10. To follow is just a brief summary of what I would include in this section for this business model. Cover the four P's: Product, Price, Promotion, and Place.]

Initially, MJD will market the jewelry in vintage clothing stores in the greater Chicago area. Our expansion plans include marketing to vintage clothing stores nationwide and placing our jewelry in museum gift shops. MJD targets shops retailing lower-priced bridge and mid-range costume jewelry.

Initial local contact is a site visit. If the owner is too busy to meet with us, we'll leave a brochure and business card at the shop. A follow-up phone call is made ten days later to schedule an appointment to discuss owner interest and selling terms.

The same methodology pertains to potential customers outside the geographic area. *The Crafts Report* magazine lists appropriate venues in their regional guide. MJD will make telephone calls to get the proper name and mailing address for the brochure, with a follow-up telephone call within seven to ten days.

The Company also has an informational Web site. As our model is to not sell directly to the end user customer, the Web site gives details about the jewelry, its historic influence, and how to buy. There is a page indicating that wholesale inquiries are welcome, including the best way to contact the Company for more information.

When the Web site is fully constructed, a press release will be sent to jewelry writers, fashion magazines, and potential customers announcing the jewelry and explaining the design aesthetic.

Plan of Operations

As this jewelry line is a logical extension of our prior line, much of the basic historic research is complete. The Company subscribes to *Variety* magazine. The filming and expected release date of period movies similar to *Elizabeth, Marie Antoinette,* and *Emma* will be monitored as new lines of applicable period jewelry are researched, fabricated, and available for sale, coinciding with the particular movie's release.

Part of the Company's long-term operational plan is to make contacts within the industry. Long-term, the Company sees itself as not only the wholesaler but also the provider of the period jewelry for use in motion pictures. To move this objective forward, the Company will submit applications to all relevant juried events to build up a listing of achievements for the Company brochure. Additionally, the Company will also keep current on local theater productions that tie into the jewelry's design aesthetic. Proof of local theater production use will build confidence in the Company's ability to perform at a more professional level.

A major consideration is the handling of Company inventory. The aim is to keep jewelry components as generic as possible so the Company can use them across design lines. This is the responsibility of the purchasing department working hand in hand with the design team.

The Company initially serves as its own webmaster. Fresh search engine copy will be written and uploaded daily. Updating the blog and pinging is a weekly task.

The home office is located in a spare bedroom. A section of an air-conditioned garage with natural lighting is cordoned off to provide work space.

Financial Assumptions

[Note: Every business plan contains an income statement, balance sheet, statement of cash flows, and break-even point analysis. I discuss how to prepare these financial records in proper accounting form in chapter 6.]

In this section is an example of the narrative that accompanies the financial statement reporting. Read chapter 6, follow my financial statement preparation instructions in that chapter, and then insert your financial statements in this section with your own narrative.

MJD plans to fund operations principally from cash provided by both gross receipts and owner investment, and will not generally rely upon external sources of financing. The Company has in place a jewelry line timed to hit the market at the same time as the 2009 U.S. premiere of the movie *Mary, Queen of Scots*. The Company feels sales of this line will provide sufficient cash flow to cover both variable and all operating expenses, with the exception of advertising, for a one-year period.

Universal Studio is in preproduction of the latest Jane Austen book-to-movie installment. Tentative release date of this movie coincides with the 2009 fourth-quarter holiday season. Due to the fortunate timing of the movie's release, the Company feels cash flow from the anticipated sales for this line of period jewelry will carry the Company at least six months, into 2010.

The Company's capital requirements result primarily from purchases of inventory, advertising, and shipping. As the inventory requirements for the jewelry line are known well in advance of fabrication, inventory cash requirements are predictable during the year.

Purchasing decisions will maintain a gross margin percentage of 100 percent. Normal jewelry markup is three times this figure. However, as MJD is a home-based business, lower operating expenses will offset the effect of the gross profit margin.

The Company also will make disciplined capital expenditure decisions, prioritized based on potential for profit generation.

Appendix

Note: The last section of your business plan is an appendix. This section should not be automatically included when you distribute your business plan. Once you start assembling the documents, you'll see that most material contained in an appendix is very personal in nature. Only release your appendix on a need-to-know basis. If you are seeking outside financing, your potential investor will most likely ask to see your appendix.

The appendix contains documents to support the facts contained in your business plan. As you write your business plan, it's helpful to note in the narrative where the applicable backup is located. For example, in the ownership section of the plan, if your business is incorporated, annotate which section of the appendix contains your articles of incorporation.

If your business plan is merely for the purpose of organizing your train of thought, and not obtaining outside financing, these documents are still relevant. Organize and place the documents in appropriately labeled file folders. I know from personal experience that the documents in question will occasionally be requested by anyone from your bank to a potential customer.

Like the rest of the business plan, the appendix is a fluid document. As your business evolves, it is natural that you'll have additional or different supporting documents. Keep your appendix updated.

As a final note about business plans, it's easy to cut corners and not write one if you're not seeking outside financing. I think this is a mistake. I compare writing a business plan to adequately studying for a big exam. We all know that sometimes you'll manage to blunder through and still get a good grade without adequate preparation for the test. However, you have a better chance of succeeding with your business (just as you would with a test grade) if you prepare thoroughly. Starting a business is a big investment of time and money. Many aspects of business success can turn on a dime. Increase your odds by preparing as much as possible.

One last point: Just because you don't need to acquire outside financing now doesn't mean you won't need to do so sometime in the future. A regularly updated business plan will simplify things when you need to put the loan request package together.

Zoning Issues

Living in a neighborhood lacking business-use zoning can be the first road-block to starting your home-based business. Luckily, with the shift toward self-employment and telecommuting, if you are not trying to secure a business license for a neighborhood manufacturing plant or car-repair business, zoning is not as much of an issue as it was in the past.

Lately, the most restrictive zoning criterion I have encountered limits the amount of vehicles visiting the home each day. Years ago, I had to draw a map of my home showing where the bathrooms and outdoor exits were located for the City of Orlando to satisfy zoning requirements.

How do you find out if your residence has proper zoning for a home-based business? If you live within city limits, start there. Live in an unincorporated section of your county? Check with your county zoning board.

Visit Your Local Municipality's Web Site

Many cities and counties have very user-friendly FAQ sections for new business owners on their Web site. Start there and follow up with a telephone call or visit to city hall to firm up the details.

If you also have a homeowners' association, it is important to check your association documents for any restrictive language.

Ignorance in this area is not bliss. It is stressful enough starting a new business without worrying about a cranky neighbor reporting you for zoning violations. Additionally, you will not be able to do any local advertising or promotions without exposing your lack of permissible zoning. Educate yourself, make alternative plans if need be, and move along.

Working around the Zoning Issues

You have three options if the regulatory agency says your residence lacks proper zoning for a home-based business:

- Request a zoning variance.
- Have an alternative business address.
- Move.

While in the zoning office doing your initial research, if you get a negative response, it is time to get information on how to secure a zoning variance. This procedure could be as simple as the city or county sending a letter to all your immediate neighbors to check for objections, to a full-blown hearing.

You might have to hire an attorney. However, if you are truly serious about making a go of your jewelry making business, this type of start-up expense is money well spent.

Using an alternative properly zoned address as your business address is a feasible alternative to the rigor of fighting city hall or your homeowners' association. Many office buildings rent mini-suites for a nominal charge. To cut costs, consider renting a business address from another business. An accountant friend of mine has this arrangement with a real estate agent. You will not need a huge space, as you will still be doing all your work at home.

There are plenty of mail-processing storefronts renting office street addresses. So what if your office is the size of a mail slot! Your workplace is at your home. Before finalizing an arrangement, make a trip back down to the zoning office to check that the potential new address is acceptable.

I suggested the third alternative—moving—tongue in cheek. It is easier said than done, unless you rent. However, if you have been looking for an excuse to move to a new residence, here is a great reason. Make sure to check zoning for your new address.

Honestly, I do not think getting zoning approval for a home-based jewelry making business should be much of an ordeal. It is a clean, quiet business bringing no increase in neighborhood traffic while adding tax dollars.

If you are interested in having a chichi secondary address, there are online businesses that rent street addresses in New York, Los Angeles, and points between. When the mail-drop business receives your mail, they scan it, shred it, and e-mail it to you via an Adobe PDF file.

Do You Need a Business License?

If you live within city limits the best place to check is with your city business license office. Otherwise, check with your county business license office. Normally, the county will require that you get your city license first if you need one. Bring it with you when you apply for your county business license. The good news is that most counties rubber-stamp your county license application if you've already gone through the licensing process with your city.

The most stressful part of this process, if you've already checked out zoning, is standing in line and writing the check for fees. However, always check what additional documents the license office needs to inspect prior to your visit. Certainly, you'll need a picture ID.

If you're incorporated, it's a safe bet you'll need your proof of filing with your secretary of state. Err on the side of caution and bring all business documents with you to avoid that repeat trip back.

Filing with Your Secretary of State

In most states this will only be a requirement if you operate under a fictitious name or have a business entity other than a sole proprietorship. If you're a sole proprietor and your legal last name is part of your business name, this usually exempts you from any fictitious filing requirements.

For example, *Maire Loughran's Jewelry Designs* doesn't need to do a fictitious filing in most states. *Designs by Maire* will. The fictitious filing form is very easy to fill out. The form asks you to provide your "real" name and address so the agency can link it to your business name. This is for the protection of the buying public.

Your state's secretary of state will most likely have a comprehensive FAQ section, and all basic filing forms for corporate and flow-through business entities will be available online. Check it out to see if you feel comfortable doing the necessary filings yourself. Otherwise, consult an attorney or one of the many online services that will fill out and file your paperwork for a fee.

Secretary of State Information

Corporations file articles of incorporation with the secretary of state. Partnerships file a general or limited liability partnership form. Limited liability companies file articles of organization.

Opening Your Business Checking Account

Start at the bank where you have your personal checking or savings accounts. You already have an established relationship with the bank and are hopefully satisfied with their service. Review their business account fee schedule. Keeping bank charges to a minimum is very important. I know my bank charges no monthly fee for its economy business account for many personal account holders. Check to see if your bank has a similar arrangement.

Simplify your life and keep the bells and whistles to a minimum for a new business. Just get the basics—the ability to write checks and make deposits. However, while at the bank, I recommend you also check out the procedures and fees to set up the following:

- Merchant account to accept VISA, MasterCard, American Express, and Discover
- Business line of credit
- Business credit cards

If you feel you need any of these additional services, evaluate the costs and benefits, shop around, and see if you can get a better deal elsewhere.

It's a safe bet that all the documents you need to apply for a business license will also come in handy at the bank while opening your account. Also, bring your business license. If you've not yet received it, bring the receipt for your business license.

Some banks don't require your business license if you've incorporated, operate as a sole proprietorship in your legal name, or have other proof of fictitious filing. As with most things in life, if you're not sure what documents to take with you, check the bank's online information center or give customer service at your branch a call.

PayPal's Virtual Terminal

Rather than paying the monthly charge for card-swiping equipment, I use PayPal's Virtual Terminal. It is amazingly easy to use. Here's how it works:

Your customer phones, e-mails you, or places an order in person (i.e., at a craft show). You collect their billing information and go online with PayPal to process the card. Like any transaction at a retail shop, where the clerk swipes your card, you know immediately if the customer's credit card is good.

Of course, you need Internet access. To fill this need, many arts and crafts venues are now providing Wi-Fi capability. I always get a signature from the customer as well by having them sign my copy of the customer receipt. If the customer is not standing in front of you, fax or e-mail a customer billing information form to the customer and ask them to return it to you via fax.

Having the customer's signature on file is merely to protect yourself in case of dispute. If you're dealing with a repeat customer, consider whether it's worth the hoopla.

In order to use Virtual Terminal, apply for PayPal's Website Payments Pro service. If you have an e-commerce site, Virtual Terminal, combined with appropriate

Virtual Terminal Contact Information

Find PayPal's Virtual Terminal informational page Web address by going to www
.paypal.com. In the Need to Accept Credit Cards section, click *For orders by phone,
fax or mail.* This page also lists monthly and per transaction fees.

shopping cart software, processes your online credit card transactions automatically. More information about how to do this is in chapter 11.

Employer Identification Number (EIN)

Do you really need one? If you're operating as a sole proprietorship and have no employees, you can use your Social Security number instead of an EIN. Sole proprietorships that have at least one employee, and all other business entities (corporations and flow-throughs) that do business in the United States, need one.

More Information About EINs

Find more information about who needs an EIN on The Internal Revenue Service SS-4 Information Page. Go to www.irs.gov. In the left navigation pane, there's a list of most requested forms and publications. If you see Form SS-4, click its link. If you don't see it, click *More Forms and Publications*. Next, click *Form and Instruction Number*. Scroll down to Form SS-4, select it, and click *Review Selected Forms*. On the second page of the form is a chart that explains who needs a Federal Tax Identification Number, in case you're not 100 percent sure.

Apply for the EIN using Internal Revenue Service (IRS) Form SS-4. This form asks for the following information:

- Business name and address
- Type of business entity
- Reason for applying (the most common answer for this section is "Started a New Business")
- Basic business type information, such as how many employees you have and what type of business you operate. For a jewelry making business, check "wholesale" or "retail" depending on target market.

Sign the bottom of the form. There are three ways to process the form with the IRS:

- Mail to the appropriate address listed on page 2 of the instructions for Form SS-4. This will vary depending on where you live.
- Fax to the appropriate number for your location (also found on page 2 of the instructions).
- Apply via the Internet to receive your number immediately.

Printed Materials for Business

Business Cards

Unless you are in the circus clown business, business stationery should be professional, clean in appearance, and free of spelling or punctuation errors. Avoid witty catchphrases and any artwork or copy that will date your printed material.

That is not to say that your business card should not be unique. Unique is good. Just stay away from unique and overly quirky.

I once made the monumental mistake of having my business name blind embossed on my business cards instead of having it printed because I thought it looked cool. This was an opinion not shared by the vast majority of those to whom I gave the card. This expensive print work was money down the drain and a job that eventually had to be reworked.

Basic printed material for a new business includes the following:

- Business cards
- Letterhead and envelopes

Some feel that business cards are an anachronism in today's world of text messaging and e-mail. I disagree. The savvy businessperson always carries a few business cards. You never know when someone will ask you what you do for a living or compliment you on a piece of self-created jewelry you're wearing.

Blind Embossing

Blind embossing is the process of raising text or designs on a surface, sort of like Braille. While this makes for an interesting border or design on printed material, it's not appropriate for text. Had I embossed the outline of a piece of jewelry on the card instead, the concept would have made for a memorable (in a good way) presentation.

Perhaps that person is a wedding planner looking for one-of-a-kind jeweled tiaras or a shop owner interested in expanding their jewelry selection. If you can whip out a fresh-looking professional business card, you've just increased your company exposure without any additional advertising expense.

Business Card Checklist

Make sure you include all available contact information, such as business name, physical address, e-mail address, Web site address, and telephone and fax numbers. If you have a logo, use it. Provide a succinct description of your product and design aesthetic. For more space, print this information on the back of the card.

For design ideas visit the business cards pool on flickr (they have some cool logos) or Ads of the World. Find both sites easily with a Google search. The specific Web addresses are also located in this book's Source Directory.

Consider the paper stock, fonts, and layout you select for your business card. Strike a happy medium between quality and price. Look over business cards you have received in the past. What aspects of the cards do you like and which are appropriate for your particular use?

Check out the following design ideas:

- Use matte silver stock if you specialize in sterling silver designs.
- Like to work with karated gold or gold-filled wire? Add a gilded edge to your card. Alternatively, use white stock with silver or gold metallic ink.
- Specialize in green or eco-friendly jewelry? Make sure you use recycled stock and that it's clearly noted.
- A jewelry artist who specializes in beading could have the image of a beaded necklace printed around the edges of the card with the clasp offset in the bottom right-hand corner.
- Another consideration is to print your business card info on a rubber bracelet. This is borderline quirky but might work for your target market.

Lastly, remember to keep your business cards functional. If they're oversized or have unusual or sharp edges, they'll be difficult to carry around with you and the recipient will more than likely find them an inconvenience and irritating. They'll end up in the nearest trash can.

When you think about creating a logo for your business, do you look like a deer in the headlights? Not to worry; not everyone can write good copy or draw a logo.

Internet Outsourcing

You can outsource many services such as graphic art and copywriting via the Internet. The procedure is quite similar to eBay. You post a project, interested vendors respond with quotes, and you choose which you prefer to work with. Feedback ratings are available so you know if you should avoid a particular vendor. Make sure the provider Web site you choose to work with has a dispute resolution department in case your project goes terribly wrong.

I've used graphic artists through the online vendor Elance in the past and was very satisfied with the quality of the work.

If you would like more information about Elance, check out L. Shepard's article on the topic at www.suite101.com. You can find the article by searching the site using the keyword "elance."

Only you can come up with the general concept for your business. If you're stuck, flip through magazines and note which logos shown in ads are appealing and which you could tailor to your business. Then sit down with a graphic artist to have a preliminary sketch drawn. Modify it until you are happy.

Letterhead and Envelopes

I don't think professionally printed letterhead and envelopes are all that crucial when first starting a business. My advice is to get the best business cards you can afford and use a word processing program to print the correspondence and company contact information at the same time, on nice paper stock that coordinates with your business cards.

Jean Hollis Weber, author of OpenOffice.org Writer, has an excellent tutorial on the Internet that walks you through the process of using OpenOffice.org to create letterhead. Follow her simple eleven-step process and you'll have a great letterhead template that even includes a logo or other graphics, if you like. Change your business address or phone number? Modify the template with a click of your mouse.

There are limited fonts available for use. Here are your three choices:

- Modern, which is a sans-serif font like Arial
- Classic, which is a monospaced font like Courier
- Decorative, which is a serif font like Times Roman

You can access Jean Hollis Weber's instructions on the Internet by doing a Google search for "create a letterhead using OpenOffice.org Writer."

Not familiar with OpenOffice.org? In use for twenty years, it's a free, easy-to-use software program that includes word processing, spreadsheets, databases, and more. Access it by going to www.openoffice.org. Unfortunately, it's not as easy to use a printer for envelopes as it is for letterhead. I recommend getting return address labels printed in the same color as your envelope, using the same font as your letterhead.

Printed material for specific target marketing such as these might also come in handy after start-up:

Flyers

Use flyers for a jewelry making business with care. For example, if you're having a trunk show of your jewelry at a local shop, hand out flyers to other stores in the surrounding areas. Offer to take some of their flyers or business cards to hand out at your trunk show for a nice cross-promotional effort.

Brochures
Brochures are thoroughly discussed in chapter 10. Brochures are very important when seeking to attract big-money customers outside of your geographic area.

Rack Cards
As the name implies, these are oversized, oblong, usually glossy cards placed in racks in hotels and the like to attract traffic to local businesses.

Recently, I've seen mini rack cards the size of a medium sticky note. They are on plain rather than glossy paper so they are probably a lot less expensive to make. Should you use rack cards? This depends on the placement of your jewelry at local shops and whether you think the rack cards will draw enough traffic to make it cost-effective.

Postcards
Many galleries use postcards to drive traffic to upcoming shows. As a jewelry artist, it's a good idea to send postcards to potential retailers to introduce yourself.

As with your business cards and letterhead, make sure there is a consistent feel among all your printed material. This goes a long way in establishing your brand or identity—a crucial aspect of separating yourself from the herd of jewelry makers.

Press Releases
I write a weekly jewelry column and I love getting press releases. There are weeks that I am staring blankly at the wall, on deadline, wondering what the heck to write about. Every writer has the same moment. That's when I go to my box of potential article ideas and press releases to get inspiration.

In fact, if a press release is timely and doesn't rehash old information about the jewelry artist, I will often bump the press release up to my most current article. So don't ever think you're being pushy or desperate by sending out press releases. However, only send releases when you have new information. If you send one out for every breeze in the wind, editors will eventually stop reading them.

Here are some press release basics:

- On a plain sheet of paper put your contact info across the top, drop down a few lines and under that type FOR IMMEDIATE RELEASE. This creates a sense of urgency.
- Lead off with a title and subtitle.
- Have a strong lead-in paragraph that gives the who, what, where, and why.
- Keep your paragraphs to three or four sentences, tops.
- In the middle, include a paragraph that quotes you as the artist discussing your product.
- Finish with a strong conclusion that gives your reader their next step. For example, go to your Web site and buy!
- Have product images available, especially if you e-mail the press release.
- End with ### to signal the end of the press release.

You've written and proofed your press release. What's next? Well, get it out there. E-mail it to jewelry writers such as myself. In the body of the e-mail, offer to provide high-res images to accompany an article or blog.

I love getting images from artists. Even though I might be writing an article about a jewelry trend or a popular-color gemstone or metal for the season—rather than a particular artist—you never know. To create interest for my readers, I always include an image of jewelry that represents the article's focus, with a link to the artist's purchasing info.

Be bold; send the press release to the appropriate editor at every fashion magazine. *In Style* magazine has a couple of great sections each month to which you can submit your press release: Shop It! Jewelry, and Deals & Steals. I'd attach the high-res images to the e-mail. The editor just might be looking for a great piece of jewelry to fill in some space that month.

Additionally, send the press release to local shops and to the appropriate editor at your local newspaper. Check out those magazines that appear at the end of your driveway or in your mailbox. If it's an appropriate venue, send a press release to them as well.

Search for online press release clearinghouses. For example, PRLog.com is a free online press release distribution service. They provide a template for your press release that includes your logo and pictures if you like. The press release will also contain a clickable link to drive traffic back to your Web site. After you create your press release, the service will distribute it to many different news organizations and search engines.

Many cities have stylishly done periodicals that are free to the public, usually available at spas, salons, and shops. While these periodicals support themselves on their advertising dollars, they are another potential recipient for your press release.

Establishing Vendor Relations

At this point, you should be familiar with many online and local suppliers of jewelry findings, components, and gemstones. If you've been purchasing retail as a hobbyist, you'll find that there's a whole new world of vendors available to you when you shop wholesale.

Maybe you've noticed that some online suppliers have both a retail and wholesale portal. Some suppliers will not sell retail. It's too much work to ship out one or two of an item.

Your advantage in establishing a wholesale account is the cost savings per unit. Most wholesalers price their product at 50 percent of retail. With efficient ordering techniques and planning, you can reduce your jewelry making cost by the same amount.

Each vendor will have slightly different requirements for their wholesale vendor accounts. One piece of documentation they will certainly ask for is your sales tax certificate or number. Wholesalers don't collect sales tax on your order. They treat your company as the intermediary between the wholesaler and the ultimate customer, who is responsible for the sales tax. This book covers applying for a sales tax number in chapter 8.

Wholesaler suppliers also have minimum order requirements. This could be as low as $100 an order to much more. Some suppliers have a minimum item per order requirement. It's your job to weigh the cost savings with volume purchasing against being able to sell enough pieces of jewelry to turn a profit.

Some wholesalers are quite picky and will only sell to established names in the jewelry making business. That day will come for you. In the interim, find suppliers with goods that come as close as possible to the components you need for your jewelry.

What about payment terms? If you're dealing with an online vendor, they accept all major credit cards, and usually PayPal as well. Local suppliers most likely take both personal and business checks with proper identification.

Some suppliers allow you to purchase on terms. In other words, you order, they ship, and send you a bill monthly. Some will ship COD (cash on delivery). I normally don't recommend either of these two payment methods for a start-up jewelry making business. If you're not home to accept receipt of the COD goods, the delivery service won't leave your order. You'll have to make alternate arrangements for delivery, adding one more item to your to-do list for the day.

It's a good rule of thumb to never order supplies unless you have the ability to pay for them. If it's easier for you to pay one invoice each month, great; see about setting up terms with the supplier. If you're attempting to delay payment, hoping your sales will create the cash flow to pay for the components, this is a slippery slope to head down. Seriously, think twice about this option.

Have the following information ready when applying for a wholesale account:

- Business name and mailing address
- Contact name, telephone and fax numbers, e-mail address
- Primary shipping address—You'll be asked if this is a residential or business address. This information is required by most shipping companies your supplier deals with.
- Sales tax number—The supplier may ask you to fax or mail a copy of the actual certificate as well.
- There is no legitimate reason for a supplier to ask for your Social Security number or EIN unless you're also applying for terms.

Remember: Each component you incorporate into a piece of jewelry ultimately affects its selling price. Manage your vendor relations to achieve as high a rate of return as possible.

Financial Planning

Throughout this chapter, I sometimes refer to jewelry as *product* and talk about per-unit profit and costs. While making jewelry is creative, you can never forget that this is a business. You have to step back from the creative process and realize that on the money-making end of this proposition, you sell a product. When it comes to financial planning, your product is no different from a computer, car, or gallon of milk.

Figuring Cost per Unit

The first step in setting a price for your jewelry is to figure out how much it costs to make each piece of jewelry. Your costs consist of many different pieces. Add the cost of each of these pieces together to come up with an estimate as to what the selling price of the piece of jewelry should be.

Raw Materials

Definitely, raw materials are an integral part of any piece of jewelry you make. However, if you purchase ten aquamarine gemstones and you use five to make the piece of jewelry, only half the total cost of the gemstone order is a cost related to this particular piece of jewelry.

This is an easy concept in principle. However, what if you buy a pound of aquamarine crystals and you use two in a pair of earrings, five in a bracelet, and set the rest aside for next month's project? Costing out the piece of jewelry starts to get more complicated.

Accounting for small findings used can be maddening. A jump ring might only cost 5 cents, but every component and bit and piece used to create the piece of jewelry adds up. If you don't factor in the price of every item incorporated into your design, you can end up selling the jewelry for less than it cost to make it.

Labor

If you have employees, labor costs must also be factored in. I find this easier than raw materials, as you pay most jewelry help by the piece rather than by the hour.

What about your labor to make the piece of jewelry? You can factor this in using a couple of different methods. After you effectively work your prototype into a wearable piece of jewelry, you can time yourself and see how long it takes you to make the piece. Divide this into your expected earnings per hour and you'll have the cost of your labor per piece.

For example, if you need to make $50 per hour and it takes you three hours to make the piece of jewelry, add $150 as your cost of labor. This is a great way to factor your own labor into the cost of the product if you are making one-of-a-kind pieces.

If you are going at it production-line style, making many pieces of the same design in an hour, I suggest using the cost of materials as your labor costs. So if your raw materials cost $10, add $10 to the price of the jewelry for your labor.

General and Administrative Expenses

Don't forget about your general and administrative expenses. General and administration expenses are those expenses you have regardless of how many pieces of jewelry you make or sell each month. The telephone company doesn't give away its service. Neither do any of your other vendors. Each and every one of your expenses has to be factored into the final price you set for your jewelry.

Review the general and administrative expenses. I've made the list as comprehensive as possible, so you may not have every one of them. For example, you'll only have interest expense if you plan to borrow money to start your business. Ditto Web site hosting; perhaps for now you plan to forgo having a Web site.

I believe it is important to have a Web presence, even if it is an informational-only site. Anyone interested in your product will pick up your Web site address from your business card and be able to find out more about your company. It's easy to refresh Web content to reflect recent changes. It's not so easy or inexpensive to reprint a brochure or reformat a business card.

Wondering about the difference between office and shop supplies? Office supplies are items like pens, computer paper, and toner—items that are universal to all offices regardless of the type of business.

Shop supplies relate more to the production of your jewelry. Some examples are buffing compounds, and pickle and cleaning solutions. These are not items you incorporate into the piece of jewelry. They are items that are necessary to *make* the piece of jewelry.

How to Cost Out Long-Lived Assets

I'd like to briefly discuss another general and administrative expense: depreciation. Depreciation is the way the cost of acquiring a long-term asset is spread over the useful life of that asset. Simply put in non-accountant lingo, what does this mean?

First, let me define a long-term asset. Normally, a long-term asset is any asset that you feel you will be able to use for one year or more. Common sense also has to play a part here. For example, I've had the trash can in my office for going on four years. Does that make it a long-term asset? Of course not, unless it was some pricey designer trash can. Many companies set a dollar limit threshold. For example, any purchase that is office supply in nature that costs under $100 is expensed rather than considered a long-term asset and depreciated. I apply the same logic to my office supplies, such as staplers and scissors.

Now, how does this apply to a jewelry making business? Let's say you purchase a flex shaft this year for $500 and figure you will use it for five years. It's not appropriate to take the whole $500 cost in the first year since you'll be using the flex shaft for another four years. Your flex shaft depreciation expense for each year is $100, or $8.33 per month.

To be able to accurately figure how much money your company made or lost, there has to be a matching of revenue to expense for that period of time. If you were to write off the entire cost of the flex shaft in year one, you would be understating net income in the first year and overstating it in all the subsequent years that you used the machine. As a small business owner, this means that you have financial figures that will not be accurate for any planning or budgeting purposes.

Depreciation is called a non-cash expense since it doesn't directly tie back to a cash outlay like other general and administrative expenses, such as telephone or office supplies. It's also a somewhat complicated topic, as there are specific acceptable methods to depreciate long-lived assets for tax return purposes. More information about the tax implications of this topic is found in chapter 8.

Pricing for Supply and Demand

Every artist has a price they would like to receive for their product. Unfortunately, many times this is not the price you can receive for your product. On the flip side, maybe your jewelry is so special and unique that popular demand allows you to set a price higher than expected.

Use Your Competition as a Starting Point

To determine a marketable price for your jewelry, look to the competition. Obviously, if you are handcrafting a helix-shaped bracelet you are not going to be able to charge Yurman prices. Check out what jewelry makers at your level of exposure charge for their pieces. In the beginning, use this as a benchmark, increasing the price as demand increases.

Also, factor in your target market's perceived value of your product. By that, I mean that if you have started making a name for yourself, or you use raw materials that are more difficult to find, you can charge more than your competition.

For example, maybe you use only untreated gemstones. There is a huge market, especially with those who wear jewelry for its healing properties, who find this appealing. Along the same lines, if you use gemstones that are hard to acquire, regardless of their cost, this also increases the perceived value of your creation. For example, while ocean jasper is extremely inexpensive, it's difficult to find vendors who stock it.

Many love a story to accompany their jewelry. If you have an attractive tag with information on the historical influence of the design or the gemstone's country of origin, this type of marketing also increases your jewelry's perceived value.

Figure a Reasonable Gross Profit

Your first step is to make sure there is a happy medium between what your target market will pay and allowing for a reasonable gross profit. I'll talk more about gross profit later in this chapter. For now, just understand that it is the difference between the selling price of the jewelry and the price of raw materials and labor to create it.

It's important to have a high-enough gross profit to cover all of your general and administrative expenses. All industries have a different standard gross profit percentage. This also differs between types of jewelry making businesses.

If you are doing strictly production-line jewelry, outsourcing all aspects of creating the jewelry, a 25 percent gross profit percentage is standard. All things being equal, at start-up, most home-based jewelry making businesses should aim for a 50 percent gross profit margin.

Putting this in dollars: If your jewelry sells for $50, then your costs to produce the jewelry should be close to $25. Ironically, most start-ups have a much lower gross profit percentage because the owner hasn't bothered to learn or does not understand how to figure a reasonable relationship between the two.

Also, I think there is a tendency to undervalue our own efforts and labor. Do not fall into this trap. Once you start giving your jewelry away through underpricing it, you are setting yourself up for failure. In the first place, you won't be generating an adequate cash flow to keep your business growing. And second, it is hard to increase prices once you are known to be in a certain price range.

Few galleries and shops will tell you that you are underpricing your goods. Meanwhile, they are elated over the increased markup on their end. However, you can expect an avalanche of protest if you attempt to raise your price to a reasonable level after the fact. After all, why would the gallery owner want to make less money selling your product than they have in the past?

Estimate Demand—Is It High Enough?

After you have figured a price for your product that allows for a reasonable gross profit, your next step is to make sure there is enough of a demand for your product to allow for an acceptable bottom line. Consider both your general and administrative expenses and the amount of owner income you want to bring home each month to pay your personal living expenses.

For example, if your general and administrative expenses each month are $200 and you would like to bring home $1,000, the total you need to cover with your gross profit is $1,200.

Next, let's figure you have a gross profit percentage of 50 percent. You need to sell $2,400 of product each month to hit your goals. This could be 240 units at $10 per unit, 48 units at $50 per unit—the possibilities are endless.

What if your financial figures just aren't working out? Now's the time to consider alternatives. For example, do you expect to have enough of a need for a particular gemstone in the future that you can boost up the volume of your order to get more of a discount on the purchase? Maybe a vendor has blue topaz on sale this month. Consider using blue topaz instead of the aquamarine that was your original vision.

Can you swap out components? For example, rather than using a fancy clasp, find one that is still attractive while costing less per unit. Maybe it's time to start looking for new vendors. Prices can dramatically fluctuate between vendors, based upon how they manage the purchasing and discounts from their vendors.

I find it's also helpful to consider return policies. Vendors that have expansive return policies allow for purchasing mistakes. Suppose you believe that a certain style necklace is going to be a big holiday item. You make a few and wait for the orders to rush in. The expected volume of orders disappointingly never happens.

As long as you have not taken the remaining gemstones or components out of their shipping containers, many vendors will accept returns for a certain period of time. Fire Mountain Gems has an unlimited, no-questions-asked return policy as long as their product bags have not been opened. I once returned clasps purchased two years previously. They immediately credited the amount on my credit card—no questions asked.

I never place an order from a new vendor without checking their return policy. When ordering on the Internet, the goods may arrive looking different from what you envisioned, or their quality might be off. It's good to know you can initiate a return if you are not completely satisfied.

Variable Costs

I've touched upon the subject of variable costs while discussing gross profit. Variable costs are those costs that in total and per unit change with the number of units sold. If sales increase 10 percent, then variable costs also increase 10 percent. Typical variable costs are those I discussed earlier in this chapter: raw materials, labor, and outsourcing.

Cost of Goods Sold and Gross Profit

Add all your variable costs together to figure up your cost of goods sold. Subtract your cost of goods sold from net sales to figure gross profit. Net sales are the total of all your sales less any customer returns.

Here's an example of how the pieces fit together:

Gross Profit Calculation

Net Sales	$1,000
Raw Materials	200
Labor	100
Cost of Goods Sold	300
Gross Profit	_$500_

I find that it's very helpful to set up an Excel spreadsheet to play around with these numbers. If you're proficient in Lotus 123 or another spreadsheet program, the basic theory remains the same. By changing cell values, you can quickly figure new pricing and costing scenarios, modifying your cost of goods sold, expected units sold, or selling price.

This is quite easy to do following these steps:

- Set up four cells with your initial assumptions. Cell A1 = selling price per unit; cell B1 = raw material cost per unit; cell C1 = labor cost per unit; and cell D1 = the number of units you hope you'll sell.
- Next, set up the Gross Profit Calculation (shown above) in a different set of cells. The formula for the Net Sales cell is A1*D1 (* represents the spreadsheet multiplication symbol). The formula for the Raw Materials cell is B1*D1. The formula for the Labor cell is C1*D1.
- Your Cost of Goods Sold cell is the total of your raw material and labor cells.
- The Gross Profit cell equals Net Sales less Cost of Goods Sold.

Once you have these assumptions programmed into your spreadsheet cells, the changes to your gross profit scenarios are limitless. If your initial assumption for number of units sold is 200, and you want to see what effect selling 300 has on your gross profit, change cell D1 from 200 to 300. Ditto the three other initial assumption cells.

I like to copy and paste the entire set of cells and label each scenario by the change effected. For example, I might label one "gross profit at 100 units" or "gross profit at $5 raw material cost per unit." Then it's easy to compare and contrast different scenarios.

Fixed Expenses

Fixed expenses are those expenses that remain the same in total regardless of how many units of jewelry you sell. All general and administrative expenses are fixed. However, keep in mind that fixed expenses per unit varies inversely. That's why it's so important to correctly estimate demand.

Not quite sure what this means? I'll give you an example. Let's say your fixed expenses total $100. If you sell 100 pieces of jewelry, fixed expense per unit is $1. Sell twenty-five pieces of jewelry and your fixed expense per unit increases to $4 per unit.

The importance of the relationship between fixed expenses and units sold will become very apparent if you examine a statement of profit and loss. As I stated earlier in this chapter, in order to continue in business, gross profit has to be high enough to support your fixed expenses.

If your salary is factored into Cost of Goods Sold—Labor, or as Officer Wages in General and Administrative expenses, your goal can be to merely break even. This means your business neither made nor lost money. In other words, you have a net income of zero.

I first introduced break-even point analysis in the Financial Assumptions section of chapter 4. Using the gross profit example from above, I'll show you how break-even point analysis plays out.

In the example, gross profit is $500. With a break-even point, your general and administrative expenses total $500 as well, leaving a bottom line of exactly zero. Many corporations actually plan for break-even point at year-end. They accomplish this goal by paying bonuses to key staff.

Use a Spreadsheet Program to Figure Break-Even Point

It's easy to format cells in spreadsheet programs such as Excel to calculate a break-even point analysis using many different assumptions.

Online directory Nourish Your Spirit has an excellent series of break-even point analysis articles showing both the cell formulas and the cell figures. It is the most understandable example I have seen on the Internet.

Access the first of four pages in this tutorial at www.nourish-your-spirit.com/breakeven.html.

Additionally, those who are really proficient with Excel can use either Goal Seek or the Excel Solver Add-In.

Tying It All Together with the Financial Statements

There are three financial statements: Statement of Profit and Loss, Balance Sheet, and Statement of Cash Flows. I'm going to walk you through each of the three, starting with the Statement of Profit and Loss.

Statement of Profit and Loss

The Statement of Profit and Loss shows all income and the variable and fixed expenses incurred in the production of that income. Some call this financial statement an Income Statement or a P&L.

The time period for this financial report is limited. For example, the twelve-month period ending December 31, XXXX, or the three months ending March 31, XXXX.

In order to effectively and efficiently run your business, you should have a basic knowledge of how a statement of profit and loss is prepared. It is a valuable tool in profitability analysis, estimation of income taxes payable, and obtaining funding for the business.

Balance Sheet

The balance sheet shows the health of a business from day one to the date on the balance sheet. Therefore, unlike the statement of profit and loss, which is for a specific time period (month, quarter, year), the balance sheet is all-inclusive time-wise. This financial statement shows assets, liabilities, and owner's equity.

- Assets are all items that bring worth to your business. Some examples are cash, accounts receivable, and inventory.
- Liabilities are all items that take away from the value of your business. A good example is accounts payable.
- Owner's equity shows your investment in the business. This investment comes from two different areas: your initial investment, and any accumulated income.

While most small business software programs automatically prepare a balance sheet, the IRS does not require that a sole proprietorship file a balance sheet with the tax return. If you operate as a corporation or flow-through, you do have to provide balance sheet figures on those tax returns.

Regardless of whether or not you are a sole proprietor, it's still a good idea to have a balance sheet handy. Other potential users of your balance sheet include other regulatory agencies, banks, and vendors from whom you are applying for credit.

Statement of Cash Flows

The purpose of the statement of cash flows is to show cash sources and uses during a specific time period. Investors and potential creditors use this information to determine whether your business should have sufficient cash flow to pay dividends or repay loans.

If I could only see one financial statement, it would be the statement of cash flows. That's because the statement of cash flows brings in most elements from the balance sheet and the statement of profit and loss, rearranging them into three different sections.

Operating

The operating section of the statement of cash flows reflects all income and expense items. Basically, any accounts you find on the statement of profit and loss are also shown in the operating section.

Investing

This section of the statement of cash flows shows all asset purchases and sales. So this section shows info from the balance sheet and statement of profit and loss.

If you purchase a long-lived asset, maybe a kiln or a flex shaft, it is reflected on your balance sheet under Assets. If you sell an asset, you'll have to remove it from the balance sheet and also reflect any gain or loss on the sale on the statement of profit and loss.

Financing

The last section shows long-term liabilities and owner equity items. For example, if you take out a loan to buy a company car, the principal amount of the loan is shown in financing, as are any future payments on the loan.

When you take money out of the company or loan money to the company, you reflect this in the financing section as well. If you have a corporation, the money you receive for any stock you sell is also added here.

Make sense? Fortunately, all accounting software packages automatically produce the statement of cash flows. If you keep your books manually, don't worry. No IRS tax form, for any type of business entity, asks for a statement of cash flows. It is merely another way for you to keep an eye on how well your business is doing.

Weathering Economic Ebbs and Flows

Whenever the economic picture seems a bit uncertain, most consumers scale back on discretionary items and are reluctant to take on any additional financial obligations. Many people do consider jewelry a discretionary item.

What can you do to recession-proof your business? It's always good to have jewelry in various price ranges. Remember earlier when I spoke about fine, bridge, and costume jewelry?

If you are operating or starting your jewelry making business in iffy financial times, keep in mind that bridge jewelry and the lower-priced fine jewelry will more than likely bear the brunt of decreased spending patterns. As a general rule, the ebb and flow of economic conditions will not have a very large impact on your wealthier customers. There will always be a market for the extremely expensive designer jewelry one sees in the chichi magazines. Along the same lines, costume jewelry in the under-$40 range will probably see little trickle-down effect from a struggling economy.

When consumer confidence is high, the sky's the limit with spending. This is especially true during the year-end holiday gift-giving season.

Keep an Eye on Discretionary Spending Patterns

The best advice I can give you is to consider the economic environment in which you exist. You don't have to be a financial wizard to do this. Just stay fairly up to date with the news. For example, it's never good when you see big retailers closing stores. Ditto the dot.com crash in 2000 and 2001. When there is a significant economic event, it will have a trickle-down spending effect.

Keep an eye on consumer debt. As consumer debt increases, there will be a point where credit card companies will start decreasing credit limits.

If there are any other consumer debacles occurring, such as a deflation of your local currency or a housing or mortgage crisis, this will affect discretionary spending patterns as well.

The wise businessperson plans for the bad times during the good. Don't frivolously spend all your profit. Never rest on your laurels. Always have a worst-case-scenario plan ready to go.

The good news is that people will always find the money to spend on items that are important to them. To that effect, I'm ending this chapter with a few suggestions on how to make money with jewelry making even during bad economic times.

Put Your Knowledge to Work

Teach classes about jewelry making. Check with local bead and craft stores to see if they need jewelry making instructors. Also, check with adult education providers and children's art schools.

If marketed properly, children's jewelry making classes are fertile money-making territory around the holidays and Mother's Day. I was flipping through a children's Egyptian art book a few weeks ago and found simple instructions to make a very cute charm bangle bracelet and earrings. Supplies for the project include empty masking tape rolls for the bangle and cardboard for the charms. With a little creativity, the project can be presented in a more-advanced fashion for children of all ages.

Teaching classes also provides an additional opportunity to generate income by selling supplies to your students. All jewelry making teachers have a supply list. If you note on your supply list that you will sell the supplies the first night of class, most students will not go through the bother of purchasing the supplies in advance. It's not unethical to sell the supplies with a reasonable markup.

Dumb Down Designs

Keep in mind that it can be easier to sell twenty-five $4 pieces of jewelry than one $100 piece of jewelry. Of course, you didn't go into the jewelry making business to sell gumball-machine jewelry; nonetheless, to keep your business alive, sometimes you've got to throttle back somewhat and sell items of lesser value.

It's good to keep an eye on preteen and teen trends. For instance, those braided friendship bracelets cost mere cents to make. Attach an interesting charm and slap on a cool label describing the metaphysical properties represented by the charm and you'll achieve a 300 percent markup.

Meanwhile, keep in the creative mode by designing and handcrafting one-of-a-kind pieces to enter into juried art shows and competitions. If you feel you lose some credibility with your cheap design line, have two different labels running under the umbrella of one company.

Pearls

Pearl restringing can be very lucrative and is very easy to do if you have a knotter. Additionally, this type of repair work will weather ebbs and flows in the economy, as your customer sees this as a necessity, much the same as a car repair.

Additionally, this is a routine maintenance expense. If pearls are worn frequently, they should be restrung at least once a year. Coming in contact with the body's natural oil causes the silk to degrade over time. It's also pretty nasty to wear a set of discolored pearls with dirty silk.

Market yourself in the proper fashion and you'll have repeat customers for years to come. This job can easily be handed off to an assistant if you are buried under with other jewelry orders.

Earrings

Earrings with multiple parts such as dangling or chandelier earrings have a tendency to fall apart over time. Most women prefer to have one earring repaired rather than throw the set away.

Depending on the type of repair and how carefully the customer saved the missing components, you may have no out-of-pocket supply expense. If you do, make sure you factor in a markup on the supplies you had to buy.

The amazing thing about this type of repair is that even if the repair costs more than the original price of the jewelry, many women will opt for the repair. The earrings may be a favorite pair, have sentimental value, or may no longer be available.

Ring Prongs

Those without soldering experience can do routine maintenance tightening the prongs on diamond and other precious and semiprecious gemstone jewelry.

Sell this to your customers by reinforcing what a stomach-dropping event it is to glance down at your hand and notice that a finger ring has dropped a gemstone. If it is an expensive diamond engagement solitaire, it's not only emotionally but also economically distressing. Imagine having to tell the husband who shelled out two months' salary for an engagement ring that you are now sporting only the band on that left-hand ring finger. Not good.

Emphasize the fact that even with careful wear, most prongs eventually loosen; it's true. Rough treatment of your hands or even snagging the ring on a garment will speed up the loosening process. However, routine prong tightening is incredibly easy to do and provides a real value to your repair customer.

If you are fortunate to have soldering skills and equipment, you can also repair broken prongs and replace lost gemstones. This is a high-profit area of jewelry repair. With expensive gemstones, many customers prefer to not leave their rings with a jeweler. If you are willing to have customers visit your home or go to their location for the jewelry repair, you will be able to tap into another source of repair revenue.

Capitalize on Your Volume Purchasing

When jewelry customers are counting their pennies and cutting back on discretionary spending, put your inventory to work for you by selling jewelry making kits. A good place to start is with gemstone-stringing kits. They are easy beginner projects and inexpensive to put together.

Most gemstone beads are sold temporarily strung in sixteen-inch lengths. Select cheaper semiprecious gemstones such as citrine, clear crystal quartz, and amethyst. Place the gem strand, two crimp beads, beading wire, and a clasp in a plastic bag and you're done.

Mark the raw materials up by 100 percent and you've made a good return on your investment of time and materials. Plus, your customer is also benefiting from this arrangement. Even with your 100 percent markup, your customer is paying less for the gemstones than they would if they bought them at a local bead shop.

Put the instructions on how to make the necklace on your Web site, and you've achieved the goal of drawing continued traffic to your site. One of these days, that traffic just might convert to a sale.

Provide Copy for Print Media

As you are probably aware, there is a plethora of magazines in bookstores on the topic of jewelry making and crafts. Being published in one of these magazines is great exposure for your business, and is a pretty darn good way to produce some extra revenue when jewelry sales are down.

Editors are always looking for beginning-level projects that will be of interest to their readers. It's easier to get published than you might imagine, but you've got to do your homework first. Read a few back issues of the magazine to see what type of projects the magazine normally publishes. Check out the magazine's submission guidelines. If the project is seasonal, plan to submit your query letter well in advance of that season.

Address the following points in your query letter:

- Sell your project to the editor. Why will their readers find this project appealing?
- Explain the materials used in the project, the skill level required, and the approximate word count for the article.
- List your qualifications.
- Enclose images of the product with a SASE if you want the images returned.
- Provide complete contact information.

Keep the query letter brief. One or two pages are sufficient. Address it to the correct editor. If that magazine doesn't show an interest, it doesn't mean it's not a viable idea; maybe it's just not a good fit for the magazine at this time. Submit it to the next magazine on your list.

Jewelry Collection Organization

As counterintuitive as it might sound, another way to increase revenue when jewelry sales are down is to help customers organize their jewelry and dispose of pieces that they have not worn in a year.

There is a lot of talk lately about the 100 Thing Challenge—simplifying life by whittling down your possessions to 100 items. Homes in the U.S. have progressively gotten larger and larger since the 1950s, and subsequently, the number of possessions it takes to fill the houses has increased as well. More rooms and closets, more furniture, clothing, and jewelry follow as the space to fill expands.

During slow economic times, your customers will also be considering alternative revenue sources. Come up with a sort of 100 Thing Jewelry Challenge advertising campaign. This can be multi-pronged:

- Offer jewelry cleaning to prepare the goods for resale.
- Advise the client about which pieces of jewelry are classics and perhaps should be retained.
- Help with the securing of a resale source.

Successful business owners can turn on a dime. Always consider alternative revenue sources that utilize your particular area of expertise.

Now that I've discussed financial planning, the next chapter of this book will discuss financial management, including handling your cash, budgeting, and extending credit to customers.

7 Financial Management

Financial management runs the gamut from handling your accounts receivable to budgeting for capital and operational expenses. This is one part of running a home-based business that you are familiar with. It's the same balancing act that you perform in running your personal household.

Banking Relationships

I recommend that you establish a good relationship with your banker. In today's world of impersonal banking, this is still pretty easy to accomplish. I know myself that I prefer the impersonal touch of doing my bank business at the ATM and online whenever possible. This is quite different from even fifteen years ago, when you would walk into your bank and most employees would greet you by name. My banker still knows me, however, because I keep all my business and the majority of my personal bank requirements at one bank.

Your banker doesn't have to recognize your face when you walk into the building, but you do need to establish a profile at the bank so that when your account number is pulled up, you will be recognized—in a good way.

Do not allow yourself to incur overdraft fees because you mismanaged your checking account balance. For goodness' sake, never rely on the float! In other words, don't write a check hoping it won't clear until you're able to make a deposit to cover the funds. That is actually illegal. When you sign a check, you are creating a contract between yourself and the recipient. The contract is that the funds are immediately available. The check is no different than handing that person cash. For that same reason, postdated checks are not valid instruments.

Obviously, the strength of your relationship with your bank will increase the longer you do business with the bank. Twenty percent of all capital infusions to new businesses come from bank loans. A good relationship with your bank will help lower any lending interest rate. That includes bank credit cards.

Another point to consider is the customer profile of your bank. Does your bank seem to try to attract large business customers? If so, you may be better served by having your business account at another bank.

A good way to enhance your business relationship with your bank is to open a checking account, and some sort of credit line or other credit account. Even if you rarely use the credit, or the initial interest rate is high, the process of approving you as a borrower clears away a lot of the due diligence involved in deciding whether to extend further credit to you.

Even if the interest rate is high, occasionally take an advance against the credit line and pay it back almost immediately. By doing this you will establish the reputation of being a prompt payer. You can always negotiate a lower rate at a later date.

Another advantage to having a good reputation with your bank is that occasionally you may have a large check to deposit and you won't be able to wait out the normal time that the money is put on hold. In that case, your bank manager may take a look at your banking profile and go the extra step to confirm the availability of funds at the payer's bank and shorten the hold period.

It's also important to shop around for a bank with reasonable fees. Many banks give reduced rates to customers with personal accounts at the bank. Make sure you read the fine print to know exactly under what circumstances you will incur a bank charge. Is there a fee for the bank to return cleared checks? With the online availability of cleared-check images, getting the actual checks back from your bank is kind of unnecessary. Some banks charge if you make more than a certain number of deposits each month. Some waive fees if you participate in online banking and direct deposit.

Managing your bank charges is just as important to your bottom line as managing your labor or raw material costs. Don't forget your responsibility to balance your bank account each month.

Balance Your Bank Statement Monthly

It's amazing how many people don't balance their bank account—or how many don't even know how to do it. I've had people tell me that they rely on the bank balance as a benchmark for available funds. This can get you into trouble. The bank only knows about transactions they have received.

The bank doesn't know about that $3,000 check you just wrote to a vendor that has not cleared or the $500 customer payment you plan to deposit later in the week. All outstanding checks and deposits in transit can dramatically influence the balance in your bank account. This in turn can affect your relationship with your banker if you have too many bounced checks due to an inaccurate bank balance.

Budgets

Preparing a budget can be tedious. After all, you may think you are just looking into the future, guessing at revenue and expense. To an extent, you are correct. However, a business with sound financial policies in place will be able to come up with a budget that is more than mere fiction.

These are the advantages to budgeting for a home-based business:

- It requires you to plan ahead.
- You are required to set definite objectives for evaluating your success.
- The budget provides an early warning to you that there may be potential problems with the way your business is operating.
- It forces you to keep tuned into all aspects of the business—not just the ones you enjoy.

To effectively budget you have to do some planning. You started this planning in chapter 4 with the preparation of the business plan. Planning and research is a constant task for any business. This applies to both your long- and short-term objectives.

Usually short-term objectives are to make a profit. Long-term, the sky is the limit. Think about what you enjoy doing and where you want to be in five years, and ten. Then update your business plan and budgets periodically to track your results.

The obvious effect of a budget should be to inspire and motivate you. As you hit budgeted figures, you'll naturally be eager to beat those projections. It's kind of hard to get motivated if you are never exactly sure how your business is doing. It's important for a home-based business to prepare two types of budgets: profit and loss, and cash.

Budgeted Profit and Loss

Okay, roll up your sleeves, get your calculator, and let's set up your income and revenue projections. The first step is to prepare the sales budget. You prepare the sales budget figures by multiplying how many units you plan to sell by the per unit price.

Wondering what is a good way to figure the units sold? Look at the advertising, the craft and trade shows you plan to attend, any customer contracts, and consider seasonal fluctuations. You can also use prior-year figures as a guideline. If you know from experience that you usually sell $500 worth of jewelry at the XYZ Christmas Craft Show, you have your figure.

This can be a guess at best when you are just starting out. You can try to back into reasonable figures by networking with your peers, although many times your competition won't be too eager to provide revenue figures. Many craft shows have revenue projections based upon prior shows available for review by vendors thinking about renting space.

Once you have tied down revenue figures, your materials and labor budget figures should be a snap to prepare. At this point, you should know exactly how much it costs you to make each piece of jewelry. Multiply that figure by the number of units you have budgeted for sale. That gives the budgeted cost of goods sold.

Subtract the budgeted cost of goods sold from the budgeted revenue figure. Voilà! You've just figured your budgeted gross profit figures. This is an easy task using a spreadsheet program. Most accounting software programs have budgeting options as well.

Your next step is to budget for your general and administrative expenses. All of these, with the exception of advertising, should be easy to estimate. Your advertising budget should not be a guess, as you should already have contacted the media of choice for advertising rates (more about this in chapter 10).

Make sure you compare your budgeted figures to actual amounts, isolate any problem areas, and make any necessary corrections. In my sample budgeted profit and loss, jewelry class revenue is under budget and shipping is over budget.

It is your job to figure out why. Regarding the jewelry class revenue, maybe class attendance was not as expected at a certain craft shop. Figure out why. Was advertising for the classes insufficient? Maybe this craft shop is just not a good venue for jewelry making classes.

Ditto the shipping. Did the overall cost of shipping go up, or did your preferred method of shipping change? Maybe you had a high-dollar order you shipped overnight, signature required. Did you pass on that extra cost to your customer? These are some examples of questions you should be asking yourself.

Cash Budget

A cash budget comes in handy when determining whether you will have enough ready cash to pay obligations as they come due. It's quite similar to the statement of cash flows covered in chapter 6, but it's easier to prepare.

Review your records and then jot down (or enter in a spreadsheet program) all of your expected cash sources and cash uses. For planning purposes, I recommend you prepare this for a ninety-day period. Of course, like all of your business-related reports, update it frequently.

Cash Receipts

Your cash receipts section contains all cash sales and collections from your customers to whom you have extended terms. You also record any additional sources of cash, such as interest, dividends, or borrowed funds.

Cash Payments

Your cash payments section contains all expected cash disbursements. This includes payments on your business credit card debt, payments on any loan term liabilities, and cash payments you anticipate making.

Just to clarify, anytime I mention cash, all forms of readily negotiable payments fall into that category. This includes checks, paper money, coinage, and other types of negotiable paper. So, the trip to the craft store to pick up some crimp beads paid for with a company check is a cash payment.

Besides the peace of mind that comes from knowing your finances are under control, why would you think it is important to have a cash budget for both the immediate period and extending out into the future? Well, planning is one reason. Another important reason is the time value of money.

Time Value of Money

Why is the time value of money so important? You use this concept to make investment decisions, such as whether to lease or purchase equipment. It's also used to make financing decisions when you don't have the ready cash to pay necessary business expenses.

You may have already done a rough estimate of the time value of money in your personal life when deciding whether to purchase or lease a car. How about when you purchased your home? This calculation is involved in making the decision for the number of years to finance.

In order to help you understand the importance of the time value of money, I'm going to lay out a very simple example my father gave to me when I got my first part-time job.

By preparing a cash budget, you'll know if there is an anticipated shortfall of cash in the future. Now is the time to plan your options. Credit card debt is one way to finance a business; accessing your business line of credit is another. Dipping into your savings is another.

This is where the time value of money comes into play. If you have a certificate of deposit earning 4 percent with a $200 penalty for early withdrawal, and a credit card with a per annum interest rate of 15 percent—which option will cost you less in the long run?

Looking at this example, it would seem to be a no-brainer that 4 percent interest income is much less than 15 percent interest payable, so cashing out the certificate of deposit seems to be the best alternative for short-term financing.

How about if you only anticipate needing the money for three months? Maybe the credit card interest will be less than the $200 early withdrawal penalty. Does this change if the credit card debt is $10,000 versus $2,000? Using the time value of money calculations will answer these questions for you.

Figure the time value of money using factoring tables. Find these in any book on investing or financial accounting. Excel has a function that will perform the financial calculations for you. Using an Excel spreadsheet, you go to Insert, Function, Financial, and pick the proper function name.

Extending Credit to Customers

The accounting term for this is *accounts receivable*. How a business manages its accounts receivable will have a huge impact on the prior subject of cash budgets.

If your home-based jewelry making business only sells online or at craft shows, you should never have an accounts receivable.

It is just common sense that credit is never extended to a one-time purchaser who you don't anticipate seeing again. A shopping cart on your Web site eliminates the need to even address this issue with your customers.

You will face this issue when you start selling to galleries and shops wholesale. All shops will attempt to purchase on credit. After all, they don't want to decrease their cash flow by paying any vendors before they have to. In essence, a shop will ask for terms so it can pay your invoice from the proceeds of the sale of your merchandise. It is entirely your prerogative if you want to operate in this fashion. I think it is wiser to always require payment upon delivery of goods.

Unfortunately, when you first start out, to get exposure in stores it may be necessary to accept customer terms. What are reasonable terms? I would like to see my

If you plan to pay $1,000 on a business loan in two years, and the money is presently invested at 5 percent, this factoring table is used to figure the value of your $1,000 payment today.

Using the table, go to the 5 percent column and drop down to two years. The factor is .9070. Multiply your $1,000 payment by .9070. You need to have $907 saved today to pay $1,000 in 2 years.

Time	1%	2%	3%	4%	5%	6%	7%	8%	9%
1 year	0.9901	0.9804	0.9709	0.9615	0.9524	0.9434	0.9346	0.9259	0.9174
2 years	0.9803	0.9612	0.9426	0.9246	0.9070	0.8900	0.8734	0.8573	0.8417
3 years	0.9706	0.9423	0.9151	0.8890	0.8638	0.8396	0.8163	0.7938	0.7722
4 years	0.9610	0.9238	0.8885	0.8548	0.8227	0.7921	0.7629	0.7350	0.7084
5 years	0.9515	0.9057	0.8626	0.8219	0.7835	0.7473	0.7130	0.6806	0.6499

customers pay in thirty days, certainly not going out past sixty days. You can also set your terms up as "2 percent ten, net thirty." This means that if your customer pays your invoice within ten days of receipt, they get a 2 percent discount. Otherwise, the entire invoice is due in thirty days.

If you extend payment terms to your customers, make sure you also address interest charges on your invoice. It is entirely standard to assess interest charges on late payments. The terms should be spelled out in both your proposal (if one is prepared) and on your invoice.

Ironically, you'll probably be extending terms to your customers at two different growth stages of your business: at its inception, when you are brand-new, and when you've made a name for yourself and are selling in volume to large outlets.

Customer Credit Applications

If you plan to extend terms to your customers, make sure you have them fill out a credit application. Here are the recommended bits of information about your client you should secure:

- The basics: customer's name, address, e-mail address and Web site, telephone and fax numbers.
- Your customer's contact person.
- Get at least three business references and call them to check out the creditworthiness of your potential new customer.
- Customer banking information, such as the bank name, address, account number, and contact person at the bank.
- Have the customer sign the credit application.
- If the customer is a corporation, insert language into the application stating that the officer who signed the application is also liable for the debt.
- It would be nice to also get a current statement of profit and loss and balance sheet.

Maybe the potential customer refuses to fill out the credit application or only partially fills it out. It's up to you whether you want to do business with this shop. Honestly, if the shop isn't willing to provide basic credit information, I would move along. It could be that they are very private, or they could be just flat out hiding poor credit. Could be their vendor supply has dried up due to lack of payment and they are seeking new avenues of merchandise. Do you think you will be the unique vendor that actually receives payment? I think not.

How to Handle Past-Due Accounts

Some customers are shameless. They will keep putting you off while asking for more inventory. I think most of us assume that everyone is as honorable and trustworthy as we are. In most cases, this is true. However, honest or not, once a customer gets behind, you are asking for more problems if you further indebt them by providing more inventory.

Send a monthly statement to each customer who owes you money. Follow up with a telephone call. You didn't go into the jewelry making business to be a debt collector, but the squeaky wheel gets the grease. The vendor who regularly and politely follows up on past due accounts will be put closer to the top of the line when the customer is issuing payments.

I wouldn't hesitate to take a customer to small claims court to collect the debt. Either this will prompt the customer to immediately pay your invoice, or you will receive a judgment in your favor that you can use to place a lien on your customer's assets. Additionally, while the debt is unsatisfied, interest continues to accrue.

This is a slightly complicated subject. To find out more about your legal jurisdiction's dollar limits for small claims court, how to file a small claims case, and collection proceedings, do a Google search using the key phrase "small claims court." Narrow down the search results by adding an identifier such as "cook county, illinois," using your personal information.

Managing Cash and the Prudent Use of Credit

You should always prioritize your cash payments. If you have terms with a vendor that includes a discount, pay that vendor within the discount period whenever possible. If you have a vendor whose raw materials and components make up a majority of your orders, it is very important to stay on good payment terms with this vendor as well.

I'm not a big proponent of establishing terms with vendors in the start-up phase of a business. It's entirely too easy to place orders for raw materials with the hope that revenue will flow in within the thirty days so you can pay your vendor. The volume discount you'll receive for placing a big order will more than be offset by interest charges if you don't issue payment in a timely fashion. Additionally, your business develops a reputation in the industry as being a slow payer. Eventually this will affect your ability to purchase on terms.

That being said, if you have a guaranteed big order from a customer, or have plans to rent a table or booth at a show with a proven track record for jewelry sales, establishing terms with your major vendors is a good idea. You'll be able buy in a high volume, lowering the cost of goods sold, and you'll be able to pay your vendor from cash receipts.

Be especially cautious if you have a history of impulse purchasing in the past. The same holds true for purchasing a raw material or component just because it is marked down. You are not saving any money if the purchase sits around your workshop collecting dust.

Cautionary Tale of Depending on Zero Percent Interest Credit Cards

Credit card companies have been pretty fast and loose with limited time zero percent interest rate credit cards for the last ten years. I agree it is quite a thrill to purchase using other people's money. However, whether it is six months or a year, these offers have an expiration date. Normally the interest on the credit card is very high, leaving you with hefty payments if you carry a balance past the expiration date.

It is quite interesting that these offers have been so numerous over the years, making it possible to move one expiring zero percent balance to another zero percent credit card for usually a nominal fee. However, just because your mailbox has been flooded with these offers in the past doesn't mean this trend will continue indefinitely. A good rule of thumb is to make automatic payments each month in an amount that will reduce your balance to zero by the expiration date.

You may wonder what's in it for the credit card company to issue these offers. The motivation is twofold: Number one, they are counting on you not paying your balance in full by the expiration date. Second, every time you make a purchase with a zero percent interest rate card, the issuing bank is still earning the merchant discount. Since you are not being assessed interest on the carried balance, there is a tendency to make larger purchases.

The next chapter expands on the topic of financial management as I discuss business taxes and recordkeeping.

8 Taxes and Recordkeeping

Establishing a simple bookkeeping system is one of those boring but necessary aspects of running your own business. As your business grows, your bookkeeping method can grow with you. In this chapter, I list three alternative methods for managing the recording of your income and expenses.

Keep Your Books Manually

I've had occasion to use this method. It's a good way to keep your records organized if they are not voluminous. One suggestion is to organize your records by having file folders for each major type of expense. For example, keep a separate file folder for sales, purchases, advertising, postage, office expenses, asset purchases, and telephone expenses.

Each month run a total for each individual expense for which you've set up a file folder. Then, staple the totaled invoices together, preferably with the adding machine tape. I also write the monthly figure on the front of the file folder. At the end of the year, it's a simple task to add the twelve months together to come up with a grand total for each category.

Prepare a summary for your tax return preparer listing revenue first, followed by expenses. Here's an example of how this might look:

Revenue	**10,000**
Purchases	**5,000**
Advertising	**1,000**
Postage	**500**
Office Expense	**50**
Telephone Expense	**200**
Profit	**3,250**

If you would like to guarantee yourself a very expensive tax return preparation invoice, use the "shoe-box" method. By that, I mean just dump all your unorganized invoices and sales receipts into a box or bag and drop it off at your accountant's office in the spring. Accountants loathe sifting through unorganized records. Maybe you do too. If so, just steel yourself for a hefty tax preparation fee.

Spreadsheet Software

If you have a computer, the chances are pretty good that you also have some sort of word processing and spreadsheet software.

Set up columns in an Excel or similar-type workbook to provide a hybrid between keeping your records manually and having a professional accounting system. I recommend listing items of revenue and expense in the first column and setting up a column for each month. As you receive revenue or expenses each month, just add the figure to the appropriate cell. This keeps a running total for each month for each category of revenue and expense.

Have a bottom-line total such as I have in the manual example and you'll have a quick and dirty statement of profit and loss for each month. Make your last column a yearly total. Print the spreadsheet at the end of the year and give it to your accountant for tax return preparation.

Harness the Power of Accounting Software

I have used all of the boxed accounting software in the under-$200 price range. I mentioned earlier that I like Microsoft Office Accounting Professional due to its stress-free tie into eBay and PayPal. If you don't need this function, the under-$200 software packages are all about the same when it comes to use and functionality. In the beginning, while your business is small, it may be easier to keep your books manually or with a spreadsheet workbook.

Many accounting software packages have a sixty-day free-trial download good for twenty-five uses. If you think an accounting software package is a good fit, try one out and see how it works for you.

Just remember: garbage in, garbage out. If the accounting software is not properly set up in the beginning, your records will be inaccurate. I also never recommend mixing personal expenses in the same setup as your business. It is too easy to mix up the records. Most accounting software packages allow for an unlimited number of companies. Set up your personal expenses as a separate "company" from your business.

Should you inadvertently mix personal and business expenses on your tax return, this will cost you big time in penalties and interest if your tax return is selected for examination by the IRS. Think the chances of an audit are remote? Think again. Since 2002, the IRS has been steadily increasing their hiring of agents. The amount of tax returns selected for audit is increasing exponentially as each agent can handle many examinations in a year.

Keeping Track of Inventory

Each year you must have accurate figures for a beginning and ending inventory of purchases made for your jewelry making business. By purchases, I am referring to only your raw materials, such as gemstones, precious metals, and components. Your beginning inventory for year one will be zero. At any one time, you will probably have three categories of inventory: raw materials, work in process, and finished goods.

I've explained raw materials above; work in process is any piece of jewelry that as of December 31 of each year is only partially completed. Finished goods are completed pieces of jewelry that have not yet left the studio.

At year-end, total each category of inventory. You then subtract this figure from purchases to come up with your cost of goods sold. In the early stages of your business, the work in process and finished goods calculation is not as critical as your raw materials inventory. The reason is that you are just not going to have a large amount of jewelry that hasn't been shipped to customers, especially at year-end right after the holiday gift-giving season.

Cost of goods sold is the amount deducted on your tax return, not total purchases for the year. Why? Well, in U.S. tax code this is just the way it has to be done. Basically, this method allows for the matching of revenue to expenses.

Do You Need to Hire a Bookkeeper or Accountant?

Judge this by time and money. If your business has just exploded and you don't have the time to deal with the recordkeeping aspect, hire a bookkeeper to lend a hand. After all, your time is more effectively spent designing and selling jewelry.

A bookkeeper doesn't have to be a full-time employee. Many bookkeepers work part-time for many different businesses. Ask friends and family to see if you can get a recommendation for a bookkeeper. Failing that, look in the Yellow Pages of your telephone book under "bookkeeping" and you'll find a plethora of choices.

Before you make a hire, carefully consider whether you can afford the expense.

Brief Example of Cost of Goods Sold

Calculating Cost of Goods Sold

Beginning Inventory	0
Purchases	1,000
Ending Inventory	400
Cost of Goods Sold	600

The cost of goods sold figure is beginning inventory plus purchases minus ending inventory. For the next year your beginning inventory is $400.

Success in your business and being able to hire help usually go hand in hand. Unless there is a real need, I think your business is better served in the beginning if you use any extra money to increase advertising.

What about an accountant to prepare your tax return? If you are a sole proprietor, look over the Schedule C, SE, and Form 4562. You use these three IRS forms to report your business net income and loss. If they look like a task you can accomplish, give it a whirl. If you have any confusion, it's best to outsource the preparation of your tax return. If you organize your records as I advise above, your tax return prep fee should be affordable.

Maybe you have done your 1040 in the past using a tax return preparation software program such as TurboTax. Just remember: These types of programs are intuitive, but if you put your tax information in the wrong place, your tax return may not be correct. This fact may or may not affect the accuracy of the amount of tax the program tells you is due.

If you have incorporated or formed a partnership, it's best to hire a professional to do the business return. These types of returns, especially the partnership return, are beyond the basic tax preparation skill level.

Collecting and Remitting Sales Tax

If you sell to the end user of your jewelry, you must collect and remit sales tax on the transaction. Okay, so who is the end user? Let me walk you through an example:

You purchase 100 sterling silver clasps from the supplier. You aren't the end user, as you're using these clasps in 100 necklaces that you're further selling to your customers. Therefore, the supplier is not required to collect sales tax from you on this transaction.

If your company sells the necklaces to a boutique for resale, the boutique is not the end user of the necklaces, so you are not required to collect sales tax from them. Now, let's say you're at a craft show selling necklaces to shoppers who are attending the show. In this instance, you *are* selling to the end user, and you must collect sales tax on the transaction. The final step in the transaction is for you to remit the sales tax you collect from your customers to your state's department of revenue.

Even if you do not sell to the end user, you will have to apply for a sales tax number because state taxing agencies require wholesale suppliers to keep your sales tax certificate number on file. You will not be able to purchase wholesale unless you have a sales tax number. Due to this fact, most states call this a "sales and use tax certificate."

How to Apply for a Sales Tax Number

Most U.S. states have a department of revenue overseeing this form of taxation. The best way to find your state's Web site is to do a Google search using the keywords "[your state] sales tax collection."

You should be able to access the registration form online. Follow the instructions to fill out the form and forward it with the fee to the appropriate address. Depending on your reporting schedule, which may be monthly, quarterly, or yearly, you report your sales information to the state and pay any tax due.

Many states allow you to file the reporting information online—a real time saver. You pay any tax due via direct withdrawal from your business checking account. Not comfortable with this method? Mail the certificate and payment to the state.

If you only sell wholesale and have a sales and use number just for purchasing, check with your state regarding what type of reporting is required. Additionally, most states do not require collection of sales tax on any purchase made in a state where you don't have a business location. For example, you operate your home-based business in Florida. You sell a pair of earrings via your Web site to an end-user customer living in Georgia. No sales tax is assessed on this transaction.

U.S. Federal Taxes for the Self-Employed

The self-employed pay two types of federal tax: income and self-employment. Income tax is familiar, as you have been paying this tax since you received your first W-2. Self-employment tax is the sole proprietor's version of the Federal Insurance Contributions Act (FICA).

On self-employed trade or business net income and certain partnership distributions, 15.3 percent self-employment tax is assessed. The self-employment tax consists of 12.4 percent for Old-Age, Survivor, and Disability Insurance (OASDI) benefits, and 2.9 percent for Medicare.

Important self-employed tax facts to remember:

- There is an income threshold for OASDI: Combined with other items, such as W-2 earnings, the OASDI portion is capped at $102,000 for 2008. The cap normally increases each year. After you have reached the income threshold, you no longer have to pay the 12.4 percent. There is no cap for the Medicare portion of 2.9 percent.
- If you file a joint 1040 with a spouse, your income threshold does not include your spouse's earnings.
- If you or your spouse has multiple Schedule Cs, for which you are the sole proprietor, total the net income/loss from all Schedule Cs for a lump sum figure (a net loss from one Schedule C will serve to offset net income from another Schedule C).

■ If your net income from self-employment is less than $400, you have no self-employment tax obligation.

What Is Net Income?

Net income from a self-employed trade or business includes all revenue received from operating the business less all expenses incurred in the production of that revenue. Some non-operating gains and losses can also be included in net income.

Under no circumstances are the following expenses deductible business expenses: the cost of the sole proprietor fringe benefits, self-employment tax, income tax, charitable contributions, or personal living expenses. Also, there is no case to be made for the business deduction of professional business attire. Uniforms are slightly different; an acceptable criterion for a uniform is the fact that it has your name/company name printed on it.

The self-employed report revenue and business-related expenses on tax form Schedule C. Carry the net income or loss shown on Schedule C to Line 12 of the Form 1040. Use the Form SE to calculate self-employment tax from the figure shown as net income on the Schedule C. You are allowed a deduction from adjusted gross income for half of your self-employment tax. Once again, this is not a business-related deduction that reduces net income. It is a deduction taken on the front page of the 1040 form.

U.S. citizens can find personal and business taxation information at www.irs.gov. The toolbar under the IRS logo has links to the personal and business sites. From those two portals, select the relevant tax topic.

Canadian? Check Out These Relevant Taxation Sites

If you live in Canada, the Canadian Revenue Agency has a very comprehensive Web site that covers all issues of taxation, both personal and business. Find it by Googling the keywords "canada revenue agency."

There are numerous articles at About.com written by the Canadian guide Susan Munroe. Her Canadian income tax tips are well worth checking out.

Federal tax depositing for the sole proprietor is done with the Form 1040ES. There are four tax deposit dates: April 15, June 15, September 15, and January 15 of the subsequent year.

Remember those monthly compilations I discussed at the beginning of this chapter? A very rough calculation for the deposit amount is figured by taking your net income and multiplying it by 30 percent. This percentage factors in the 15.3 percent self-employment tax and assumes you are in the 15 percent federal income tax bracket.

If your tax bracket is higher or lower, adjust the 30 percent accordingly. If you or your spouse (if married and filing a joint return) also receive W-2 income, factor these figures into the equation as well.

Tax Code Can Be Baffling, So Checking with a Professional Is a Good Option

I could write an entire book on the topic of taxation. Only the basics of U.S. taxation and reporting are covered in this chapter. Consult with your accountant or tax return preparer for more information.

You can also call the IRS at (800) 829-1040, or visit your local taxpayer services office for more information. While calling the IRS or during your visit, ask for the Form 1040ES package.

This package is also available via download at the IRS Web site. The Form 1040ES is one of the IRS's most requested forms. At the IRS home page, check the left-hand toolbar. You will see a direct link to this form and complete instructions on how to fill it out.

Deducting an Office in the Home

If you regularly and exclusively use a portion of your residence for your jewelry making business, you can take an additional business deduction for this use. Calculate this deduction by dividing the amount of your home used for the business by the total square footage of your home. This gives you your business-use percentage. Multiply related expenses by this percentage to figure out the deduction amount.

Here are some examples of deductible home office expenses:

- If you own your home: mortgage interest and real estate taxes
- Rent paid to a landlord other than yourself
- Lawn care
- Maid service
- Utilities: Be careful when deducting your utilities. Unless you are operating a manufacturer plant in your home office, the utilities you deduct should never be more than 10 percent. Why? Well, think about the amount of energy the appliances in your home use and consider how much power you actually use in the home office. It is disproportionate.
- Repairs and maintenance

Note that I did not include telephone expenses. You cannot deduct a portion of your personal telephone line as a home office expense. You either have a 100 percent deduction for a dedicated business line or no deduction at all.

I'm going to walk you through an example of how to calculate the other expenses. You pay a maid service $100 a week to clean your entire home. Your home office percentage is 20 percent. You can deduct $20 of the maid service fee on the Schedule C as a business expense.

As with any business-related expense, keep the maid service invoice or proof of payment for three years after you file your tax return. I recommend you file invoices of this nature in the monthly file folder with your other business invoices.

If you own your own home, I never recommend taking the home office deduction. The reason for this is simple. The two largest deductible expenses, mortgage interest and taxes, are already deducted 100 percent on the Schedule A. It's not worth the trouble to muddy up your tax return by splitting the expenses between the Schedule C and the Schedule A.

I once added a room to my home to use strictly for a home office. Even then I did not take the home office deduction. Why draw attention to your tax return by taking a deduction that you can take on another tax form?

If you rent, it is a totally different story. What a fantastic deduction! If your monthly rent is $1,000 and your home office percentage is 10 percent, you can deduct $100 of your rent each month as a business-related expense.

Taxes and Hiring Jewelry Making Help

The big question every small business owner asks about hired help is whether the person needs to be an "official" employee or whether the person can be an independent contractor. This is a simple matter of control. Do you control how and when your help performs their job? Do you supply the materials to complete the job? Does your help work just for you, or do they work for many different businesses?

If you require your help to work certain hours, regardless of whether you pay them by the hour or by the piece, then your help should probably be considered an employee. Ditto if you provide the materials for them to do their job, or if you provide them with benefits such as health insurance.

If your help provides their own materials and you give them a deadline for completion, rather than requiring they work certain days or hours, then your help should probably be considered an independent contractor.

This is a very important issue. Proper classification of workers can be confusing, but it's crucial to get it right. You might be wondering why this is such a big deal. Well, if your worker is an employee, you are required to prepare a proper paycheck, match certain employment taxes, deposit the employment taxes on time, and give the employee a W-2 at year-end. This is a lot of work and it takes time to do it correctly.

Now compare this to a worker who is an independent contractor. You give them a check for services rendered, with no need to withhold or deposit payroll taxes. Your only other requirement is to give them a Form 1099M if you pay them more than $599.99 in one calendar year.

Weighing the difference between the treatment of the two, it's easy to see why many small businesses opt to pay help as independent contractors regardless of whether the classification is correct. Don't be tempted. Misclassification of workers will cost you big time in penalties should the IRS catch up with you.

Properly Classify Your Help

The IRS has an excellent information page about this issue. Find it by going to the IRS Web site at www.irs.gov and using the keywords "independent contractor or employee" in the site's search box.

The page further elaborates on the three key elements of control: behavior, financial, and type of relationship.

If after reading the information you're still not sure about classification, follow the instructions to file Form SS-8, Determination of Worker Status for Purposes of Federal Employment Taxes and Income Tax Withholding.

This page is a one-stop shop, as you'll find links to the proper reporting forms for employees and independent contractors at the bottom of the page.

How to Deduct Vehicle Expenses

You can use one of two methods to deduct vehicle-related expenses:

Standard Mileage Rate (SMR)

Accounting for your business vehicle use could not be simpler if you use this method. Keep a notebook or a mileage logbook purchased at an office supply store in your car. Every time you get into your car for business purposes, just note in your log your car's beginning odometer reading and briefly annotate the purpose of the trip (for example, see XYZ client, go to bank, buy office supplies).

When you return to your home office at the end of your business trip, note the ending odometer reading, calculate the total miles driven, and you are done. So if your beginning odometer reading was 10,521 miles and your ending odometer reading was 10,530 miles, your total business miles for this trip totaled 9 miles. I recommend writing this figure in its own column, set off to the right-hand side of your log, so you can quickly total all trip miles.

There is no need to track any sort of personal use of the car. Therefore, it will not seem odd or unusual to see gaps in the ending odometer reading for one business trip and the beginning odometer reading for the next business trip.

The standard mileage rate (SMR) is used to approximate most expenses incurred with the use of a vehicle. For example, gas, vehicle insurance, oil changes, and other repairs and depreciation. To make this abundantly clear: If you use the SMR you *do not* also take a deduction for gas, insurance, repairs, and maintenance or depreciation.

However, you can claim some other vehicle-related expenses in addition to the SMR. These include tolls and parking expenses you incur while on a business trip, and the business percentage of interest paid on a car loan.

To calculate the business percentage for your car, write down your odometer reading on January 1 and deduct that number from your odometer reading at December 31. That will give you the total miles placed on your car for the entire year. Then figure the percentage of business miles you placed on the car.

For example, on January 1 the odometer reading was 10,000 and on December 31, the odometer reading was 20,000. You placed 10,000 miles on your car during the year. You total all of your business miles using the method I outlined above, and that figure was 5,000. Your business percentage is 5,000 miles/10,000 miles, or 50 percent. You can take a business deduction for 50 percent of the interest paid on your car loan.

At the end of the year, multiply the total business miles you have placed on the car by the standard mileage rate published by the Internal Revenue Service and you have your SMR write-off. Due to the escalating cost of fuel, the standard mileage rate has been increasing each year for the last few years. Add your business tolls, parking, and car loan interest to this figure for your total vehicle business expense.

Actual Cost Method

The second allowable method is the actual cost method. Actual cost and not SMR must be used if your business has more than four cars, or leases cars (see your tax accountant for other exclusions).

This method also requires the use of an auto log. Figure the business use of your vehicle the same way as with the SMR method. Once you know your business use percentage, most expenses incurred in keeping that vehicle on the road during the year are multiplied by that percentage to figure your auto expense write-off.

One notable exception to this rule is any repairs or renovations made to the vehicle that substantially increased its useful life. For example, routine maintenance such as oil changes or new tires are classified as repair items and expensed in the year incurred. Add the expense of big jobs, such as rebuilding your transmission, to the basis of the vehicle. It is then depreciated rather than expensed in the year the cost occurred.

Tax code variances make depreciating a vehicle a complicated topic. Vehicles are subject to yearly depreciation limits, which can vary based upon the type of vehicle. For example, if your company vehicle has a gross vehicle weight over 6,000 pounds, it is depreciated in a different fashion than the owner's Mercedes.

You record depreciation on IRS Form 4562. Read the instructions for the form. If you are unsure about how to depreciate your company vehicles, consult a tax return preparer or your accountant.

Walking through an Example Using the Actual Cost Method

You have totaled all your vehicle-related receipts. During the year you paid $1,500 for fuel, $1,200 for insurance, and $120 for oil changes.

Per your mileage log, your business-use percentage is 75 percent. The allowable business write-off is $2,115 {($1,500 + $1,200 + $120) multiplied by .75}.

And please be perfectly clear on this point: standard mileage rate is not taken in addition to actual cost. It's one or the other, *not both*.

Business versus Hobby for Tax Reporting

If you operate as a sole proprietor, partnership, or S-Corporation to be able to write off your jewelry making expenses, your work has to be regarded as a business rather than a hobby. The IRS has strict criteria as to the definition of a hobby versus a business. Straight-up corporations are not subject to the IRS's hobby loss rules.

Basically, you'll meet the business versus hobby criteria if you turn a profit three years out of the last five tax years. It doesn't have to be a tremendous profit to satisfy the business intent criteria. Let's face it: If your jewelry making business is not turning a profit, what's the point of operating the business? Few people go into a business thinking they will lose money. Here are other criteria for judging the seriousness of the jewelry making business intent:

- Does the time and effort you put into the business show you are attempting to make money?
- Do you have some prior experience or education in the jewelry making field?
- Are you planning to live on the net profit from the business?
- Have you made a profit in a similar business in the past?
- If there are losses, is it because you are in the start-up phase of the business, or perhaps due to circumstances beyond your control, such as being located in a weather-related disaster area?
- Are you changing the way you operate the business to move into a profit position?

Reclassification to Hobby Losses

You might be thinking, Why does the IRS care if my small business makes money? Well, it goes beyond the business tax–collecting standpoint. If you're operating as one of the business entities I mentioned previously, any business loss serves to offset other items of income you show on your Form 1040.

For example, if you or your spouse also has W-2 wages, a loss for the jewelry making business will reduce the amount of taxable wages. This has been an area of abuse in the past as people set up sham businesses to take a loss.

I knew a woman who operated as a sole proprietorship selling makeup. Well, you guessed it; her only client was herself. It's a nice gig to try to write off personal living expenses as business losses, but it's against tax code. So what happens if the IRS audits your tax return and sees that you have losses more than three of five years, considers the other bulleted criteria, and reclassifies your business losses as hobby losses? Well, it's not good. All of your gross income is taxed, while your expenses in the production of that revenue are greatly reduced.

You itemize hobby expenses on Schedule A. If you don't have enough other deductions to itemize, you've lost the expense deduction. You are also not allowed to deduct hobby expenses on the Schedule A exceeding your gross hobby receipts.

For example, say your jewelry making customers pay you $1,000. Your raw materials and office expenses total $1,200. You are limited to deducting $1,000 in expenses. However, take this fact into consideration: You are not reading this book if you want to pursue a hobby or dabble like an amateur. You want to turn your hobby into a profit-making business.

Advertising might eat up your profit in year one; I know it did for me. After year two, you should have fine-tuned your start-up and be moving into a real profit position. You always need to keep an eye on the future and track trends that will affect the jewelry making business.

However, if you haven't started making a profit in the first two years, you need to go back to the drawing board and figure out why. It shouldn't take the risk of an IRS audit for you to realize that something about the way you are doing business is not working.

Jewelry Making Legal and Ethical Issues

Protecting Your Work

Trademark

A trademark is a unique symbol, word, or phrase that identifies your product. Two symbols designate a trademark. One is ™ and the other is ®. Of the two, only the ® indicates that a formal registration with the U.S. Patent and Trademark Office (USPTO) has been completed.

An example of a trademark is Coke® or Whopper®. There are two basic criteria for obtaining a trademark. The first is to do a search at USPTO to make sure your preference is not already trademarked. Second, you cannot trademark a phrase that is common in ordinary speech. For example, Coke® is one example of a soda or carbonated drink. While Coke® can be trademarked, *soda* or *carbonated drink* cannot.

Example of a Jewelry Maker's Trademark

Tiffany & Co. featured designer Elsa Peretti not only trademarks names for her designs, she also has a trademark on her actual name. On the Tiffany and Co. Web site, she is referred to as Elsa Peretti®. One of her trademarked jewelry designs is Diamonds by the Yard®.

None of the words making up the phrase *diamonds by the yard* is all that unique. However, the phrase itself is; hence, the issuance of a trademark.

So, if you have a really cool business name or want to protect a term by which you refer to your product, a trademark is the way to go.

How to Get a Trademark

After you have confirmed that no one else owns a trademark on your symbol, word, or phrase, you file an application with the USPTO (www.uspto.gov). The application can be done online using the Trademark Electronic Application System (TEAS). From the main page, you can access the TEAS home page by doing a site search using the keyword "TEAS." I highly recommend you click the *Where Do I Start* link on this page and read all of the provided information thoroughly before you begin.

The instructions accompanying the application are quite lengthy. Pack a lunch and get yourself in a patient state of mind prior to beginning the application. Also, be prepared to part with the $350 application fee.

Copyrights

Copyrights protect original artistic works and the written word. You may want to copyright any unique description you have for a piece of jewelry. A copyright also comes in handy if you have a Web site and wish to keep others from copying and pasting your copy into their own sites.

This happened to me a few years back. I had a habit of writing descriptions for product and uploading it to the Web so I could tweak the copy and image presentation. Many times the copy went up initially with horrendous typos that I fixed as part of the editing process.

I was checking inbound traffic one day and clicked on a link coming in from a competitor's site. Well, they had snitched a few of my product descriptions—typos, run-on sentences, and all. It was actually quite funny. I was too busy at the time to pursue it, but most Web site owners vigorously go after these types of theft.

How to Get a Copyright

The U.S. Copyright Office site (www.copyright.gov) is a well-written, easy-to-understand source for all information regarding copyrights. From the home page, I suggest you first access the *Copyright Basics* link located in the About Copyrights section. This links takes you to a twelve-page PDF file that goes through, among others, the following topics:

- What is a copyright
- Who can claim a copyright
- What works are and aren't protected by copyright

- How to secure a copyright
- Notice of copyright
- Length of a copyright
- How to register your copyright

Getting a copyright is a very stress-free procedure. Once you have created an original literary, dramatic, musical, or artistic work in fixed form, you've automatically secured a copyright. Let me repeat that: Your copyright is secured immediately upon creation of your original work. No other legal filing is required.

Notice of Copyright

While it's not necessary to secure copyright protection, the following notice can be added to each original work:

The copyright of the article "Jewelry for Children" is owned by Maire Loughran. Permission to republish "Jewelry for Children" in print or online must be granted in writing by the author.

The use of a copyright notice is not required under U.S. law. However, I think it's always a good idea to add a similar blurb to the bottom of each and every page you upload to the Web. For some reason, many people don't realize it's plagiarism if they use your copy or images posted on the World Wide Web.

Length of a Copyright

The life of any copyright is usually the life of the author plus seventy years. That's why certain songs and pieces of art are now in the public domain, freely used by anyone. One well-known example of this is the "Happy Birthday" song, which fell into public domain in 1991.

Another example is pop artist Robert Indiana's famous LOVE logo. He created the logo in 1965 for a Museum of Art Christmas card. Unfortunately, the automatic copyright feature did not come into existence until after 1975. So now, everyone and his brother can freely use this iconic logo.

Why and How to Register Your Copyright

You may be wondering why anyone would go through the fuss of registering a copyright. There is one simple reason: You cannot file a copyright infringement suit in the U.S. court system without said registration.

You can register your copyright online through the electronic Copyright Office (eCO). The link to this service is located on the home page of the U.S. Copyright Office. Clicking the *Electronic Copyright Office* link will take you to the online system. I suggest you read the eCO Tips and FAQ prior to filling out your application. The good news is that the fees to register a copyright are quite modest.

Before I move on to the topic of licensing, I want to discuss one other copyright issue: What happens when you work on a commissioned piece of jewelry? Do you or your customer own the copyright on the jewelry design?

Unless you transfer rights of ownership when you complete the transaction, you own the copyright. To further protect yourself, you can add a blurb to your invoice, stating, "Copyright remains with [your company name here]. This sale does not transfer copyright."

Licensing

Another legal issue you may encounter as a jewelry maker is licensing your designs. This occurs when you enter the world of manufactured, mass-produced jewelry designs. Let's say you have a trademark for a bracelet you call "The Wrist Adorned" and you have some really killer copy (copyrighted) detailing how this bracelet is based upon a design worn by Marie Antoinette.

One day you are sitting in your home office flipping through jewelry making catalogs when you get a telephone call from a manufacturer wanting to license your bracelet. There are many different issues you need to address when licensing your design.

- Approval of the quality of the product
- The right to artist credit
- The right of ownership of the original work
- How you will be paid—flat fee or royalty
- Determination of the financial terms of any royalty
- Artist's rights to termination

It is very helpful to get the help of a trained professional to review any licensing contract before you sign it. Legalese can be very confusing to the layperson who doesn't deal with it on a daily basis. It's well worth the legal fee to have a disinterested third party check the document for any unfavorable clauses.

Get Legal Help Online

There any many online services that will direct you to an attorney in your area who handles licensing, trademark, and copyright issues.

You'll be asked to provide information such as your geographic location, desired skill level of the attorney, and how you wish to pay. Then you'll be asked to describe your case. Interested lawyers in your area will respond with their plan of action and fee, and you choose the one you like. Make sure you select a service with a satisfaction guarantee.

One of the larger services is Legal Match. However, you can find many others by doing a Google search using the key phrase "legal help [your state name here]."

Fighting Infringement

If you find that someone is using your trademarked or copyrighted work, the first recommended step is to contact him or her. Many times this will cause them to cease and desist. After all, they probably know they are doing something wrong, and just the threat of a lawsuit will be enough to make them stop.

How about if their use of your product is notorious and they have made a good bit of money using your idea? It may well be worth a lawsuit to make yourself whole. After all, your competitor has not just been stealing your ideas; they've also been stealing your potential sales for the like product.

Like all lawsuits, you must weigh the costs against the expected gain. If you watch any of those court television shows, you know that many times the amount in questions is *de minimis*. The plaintiff sues because of principle; they don't necessarily care about the damages awarded. That's fine in small claims court. However, when you are hiring an attorney who doesn't work on a contingency fee, you should have realistic expectations about being awarded a judgment, and being able to collect on that judgment.

Famous Designers Do Fight Knock-Offs

From what I read in the trades, David Yurman keeps his legal team occupied full-time fighting his jewelry design knock-offs. I read an article in the February 2008 edition of *W* magazine on the topic of clothing designers maybe getting too much inspiration from their fellow designers.

It does seem that once a trend is established for a season, all the designers show variations of the same theme. Is that a bad thing? How close is too close when it comes to replicating design ideas?

Clothing and jewelry designer Vera Wang was quoted in the *W* article as saying, "Nothing has never been done before . . . we're still working within a certain structure."

I agree. The use of untraditional materials in jewelry designs is just about the only way to truly get a new spin on the old designs. However, just as you are outraged if someone duplicates your jewelry, celebrity jewelry designers feel the same. Don't come too close to replicating another's work and risk being sued yourself.

Always seek the help of an attorney if you have any questions regarding licensing, copyrights, or trademarks.

Insurance for the Self-Employed

General Liability

Jewelry just doesn't lend itself to product liability suits in the same way as edible and other types of products. Unless you have razor blades or poison incorporated into your design, the requirement for product liability insurance is usually minimal.

However, what if a customer visits your workshop and hurts themselves on a piece of equipment, or a retail customer sues you for breach of contract after you only delivered ten brooches instead of twenty in time for the Kwanza holiday gift sale? What if one of your bracelets breaks and your customer's child chokes on one of the components? Then, there is the aggressive business suing you for copyright infringement because they think your peridot earrings are identical to theirs. Maybe the suit is frivolous, but how much will it cost you to get to that decision?

One thing to remember is that your homeowner's insurance probably does not cover you for any of these horrifying dilemmas. It is always in your best interest to check out various business insurance options to augment your homeowner's or renter's insurance.

Check out a hybrid type, also known as "in-between insurance," which covers only business-related issues, leaving the coverage of your home and belongings under the jurisdiction of the homeowner's policy. There are also blanket policies available, offering $1 million of coverage if you are sued personally for any reason.

Your choice of business entity also plays into this decision. If you are incorporated and the business is sued, usually only business assets can be attached to satisfy the suit. After all, the main reason for incorporation is the limited liability aspect of this type of business entity.

This is an important issue. Your first step is to check with the agent who handles your homeowner's or renter's insurance. See what is and is not covered. Ask for a recommendation for a business insurance agent. Describe your business to this agent and ask them for coverage suggestions. If you had an attorney set up your business, get in touch with them first and have them go over all the liability aspects associated with your business.

Casualty and Theft Insurance

Your business inventory and tools probably do not have coverage under your homeowner's policy. Additionally, consider what happens if finished jewelry or supplies are stolen from your car or hotel room while you are attending a trade show.

Once again, the best advice I can give is for you to check with your insurance agent to see what coverage limits exist. If you anticipate transporting any type of business material or supply in your car, I would do the same with the company handling my vehicle insurance.

Obviously, you limit the hoopla over casualty and theft insurance if you merely keep a few hundred dollars' worth of supplies around your home at any one time. Do a cost-benefit analysis, weighing the additional cost to insure against casualty and theft losses against the probability that you will incur such a loss.

Health Insurance

If you or your spouse have outside employment and have coverage through that employer, securing health insurance is not a concern for you at this time. Keep the information in this section in the back of your mind for the time when your business grows to a point where you can quit your day job to work for yourself full-time.

Unfortunately, if you don't have a large company behind you, negotiating benefits, you can end up with high insurance premiums and high deductibles, with less coverage. Preexisting conditions—forget about it!

One option is to align yourself with another group. Maybe you are a member of American Association of Retired Persons (AARP) or an artists' guild. Check with them for any group health insurance coverage packages they provide to members.

For example, if you are a member of Freelancers Union, you are eligible to join their group for health, dental, and life insurance. You are also eligible for discounts at the YMCA, Staples, Barnes & Noble, Hyatt Hotel, T-Mobile, and more. Best of all, membership in the Freelancers Union is free.

Per the Freelancers Union Web site, more than 30 percent of U.S. workers are self-employed. With your membership in Freelancers Union or another artists' guild, you align yourself with a large group that is better able to negotiate affordable rates.

Health Savings Account

You can also consider setting up a health savings account (HSA). Those that have coverage under HSA-approved high-deductible health insurance plans can also start a HSA. Okay, what does this mean in plain language? If you have health insurance with a high deductible (and the plan meets the criteria of HSA), you can set up an HSA as a bridge between what you spend in medical costs each year and your deductible.

For example, after my husband died back in the 1990s, I had only catastrophic medical coverage. Before the benefits kicked in, I had to incur at least $5,000 in medical expenses in one year. I had coverage for both my son and myself, so that was $10,000 in total deductibles.

President Bush passed the HSA bill in 2003, but had it been in existence back in the 1990s, I could have put money into an HSA to cover any of my medical expenses up to the $10,000 deductible. It's a form of self-insurance.

So what's the advantage to setting up an HSA? The good news is that the money you put into an HSA serves to reduce your taxable income, dollar for dollar. HSA is a Form 1040 page 1 deduction from adjusted gross income. All things being equal, if your self-employment income is $20,000 and your contributions to an HSA are $2,000, your adjusted gross income is $18,000.

Another high point is the fact that it is portable. Unlike a Flexible Spending Account, the balance in the account (including the income) carries forward indefinitely. You do not have to use all of your yearly contributions in that same year. Even better, the HSA earns income just like your money market or savings account. Your contributions are not sitting idle if you do not immediately use them. They are working to create passive income for you.

Once you are no longer enrolled in an approved plan, or if you are covered under Medicare, you are no longer eligible to contribute to an HSA. You are only taxed if you take money out of the HSA that is not used for medical expenses.

The rules for using a Health Savings Account are voluminous. Check with your accountant or with the IRS at www.ustreas.gov for more information about the tax benefits of an HSA. Find the exact pages by doing a site search using the keyword "HAS." Online health insurance instant quotes for HSA-eligible plans are available at www.hsainsider.com.

Health Insurance Resources

Check out these organizations for more information about self-employed health insurance:

Craft Emergency Relief Fund (CERF)

CERF is accessed at www.craftemergency.org. Do a site search using the key phrase "health insurance." This brings up a link to a very interesting special report about health insurance.

Fractured Atlas

Fractured Atlas has years of experience working with health insurance companies and health-care providers, and they work as the member's advocate. Unfortunately, Fractured Atlas only has health insurance allies in twenty-seven of the fifty U.S. states. They also provide information about how to secure nonperforming artist general liability insurance. Individual membership is under $100 per year.

Their Web site is located at www.fracturedatlas.org. On their home page, click *Programs & Services* on the horizontal toolbar. Follow this link to more information about health and liability insurance.

Required Gemstone and Metal Legal Disclosures

If you are doing business in the United States, the Federal Trade Commission (FTC) mandates that you use certain legal notices regarding your jewelry product. These notices are meant to protect the consumer from deceptive advertising of jewelry and jewelry-related products, and run the gamut from gemstone treatments to what items can be labeled as handcrafted. Beside the fact that the FTC mandates these disclosures, it's just good business to do so.

Precious Metals

There are certain requirements as to what you can label as sterling silver, karated gold, or platinum.

Sterling Silver

In order to advertise a piece of jewelry as being sterling silver, it must contain at least 925/1000ths pure silver. If it does, the proper marking is SILVER, SOLID SILVER, STERLING SILVER, OR STER.

This qualification precludes you from describing a silver-toned component as "silver" if it is not sterling silver. I don't often use base-metal components, but when I do, I include a description such as "base metal silver-toned clasp" (or whatever the component might be).

Karated Gold

Karated gold is very expensive, but there are times when you just cannot use a substitute. Sometimes, to satisfy your design aesthetic, you need to hammer the metal. It is a dicey proposition to hammer gold-filled wire or sheet; you probably will have to use karated gold to achieve the effect you desire.

All gold castings start with pure 24-karat gold. If used in jewelry, the pure gold is mixed with an alloy to provide the strength needed for continued wear. These alloys may be copper, zinc, silicon, nickel, silver, or boron, to name a few. The alloy used will also vary based upon whether it's yellow, white, or rose gold.

You cannot use the term *gold* without modification for any product that is not

24 karat. Some of the modifications, which are the result of the addition of alloys, are 10K, 14K, or 18K. Normally you will not have to worry about the correct designation, as your suppliers will have already labeled each product (that you are using as raw material) as to its gold content; you simply use the same designation.

Gold-Filled Jewelry

Gold-filled jewelry is a hollow tube of usually 14K gold (sometimes 10K is used) that is filled with another metal. The exterior of the gold-filled jewelry—everything you can see or touch—is a solid layer of karated gold.

This tube of karated gold is approximately 100 times thicker than gold plate, and is made by bonding with heat and pressure. With normal wear and tear, the karated gold will never tarnish, chip, or wear off. By law, this layer of karated gold has to be at least 1/20 of the total weight of the metal portion of the piece of jewelry.

In the United States, this process is referred to as "gold filled." In Europe, the same process is called "rolled gold." Both terms are synonymous. Many jewelry purchasers outside the jewelry trade mistakenly think "gold filled" is the same as "gold-plate." Gold-filled is a higher-quality product.

Platinum

Not many home-based jewelry makers dabble in platinum. It's just too expensive. Keep in mind for the future that a product must be composed of at least 950/1000ths pure platinum to be labeled as such.

Plated Gold

There is no legal requirement for the amount of gold that is "plated" over the base metal.

Hallmarks

Any manufacturers selling karated-gold jewelry must designate its purity and stamp the ring with their hallmark (a unique symbol for their business). This hallmark and designation are usually placed on the underside of the jewelry and will be in extremely small script.

Get out the magnifying glass for this one. If you're married, check out the inside of your wedding band to see what I'm talking about. If not, any karated gold ring will have the same stamping.

The same is true for sterling silver. I've had my own designs cast into sterling silver charms. The casting company will ask how you prefer the sterling silver annotation to be shown—for example, .925 or STER.

Implications for your home-based jewelry making business? This is another keep-it-in-the-back-of-your-mind moment. All karated gold and sterling silver components you purchase should be designated as such. You won't have to worry about these requirements until you build your business into a manufacturing concern. Don't laugh; you might end up doing extensive production-line jewelry.

Handcrafted

It is unfair or deceptive to represent, directly or by implication, that any jewelry product is handmade unless the entire shaping and forming of such product from raw materials and its finishing and decoration are accomplished by hand labor.

Does this mean that you can't describe your jewelry as handcrafted if you buy ready-made clasps? No, not at all. As long as you affix the clasp to your necklace or bracelet using human rather than machine labor, you are handcrafting the jewelry.

The big hoopla about this is the fact that your average customer will pay more for an item that is artisan-handcrafted than one that shoots out of a production-line machine system because they are paying for the romanticism of the jewelry artist sitting in their studio in the country, creating the jewelry with love. Okay, maybe a bit of hyperbole, but that's what it boils down to.

Consumers have long had a love affair with handcrafted items, whether it is jewelry, furniture, or haute couture gowns. The FTC wants to make sure they get what they pay for.

Pearls

Pearls are not gemstones. Like amber, coral, and jet, pearls are a by-product of a living creature. Natural pearls formed by mollusks are no longer readily available. All pearls currently available (retail) are cultured by placing a small piece of shell into a living oyster. This irritates the oyster, causing it to produce nacre (a white lustrous coating) around the shell fragment. Over time, the nacre builds up, and voilà—a pearl.

A big no-no when marketing any pearl jewelry is to call it *natural*. Any readily available (and affordable) loose pearl is cultured. Avoid misrepresentation and label your jewelry such.

Most home-based jewelry makers use freshwater pearls or glass pearls.

Freshwater pearls are cultured in lakes and rivers in China, and, to a lesser extent, in the United States. Freshwater pearls are sold in many different shapes: nearly round, potato-shaped, teardrop-shaped, and rice-shaped, to name a few, and they are extremely inexpensive.

Bleaching is common to present a more-pure white color. So is dyeing. Some commonly found colors are peach, pink, lavender, and peacock (a cost-effective alternative to Tahitian pearls). If the pearls you use in your jewelry are bleached or dyed, make sure you add that qualifier to its description.

If you are using peacock-colored freshwater pearls, do not advertise them using the term Tahitian. They may come close to looking like Tahitian pearls, but they most certainly are not. The Tahitian government limits the exporting of its pearls to those that have at least .8 mm nacre thickness. To advertise your freshwater pearl jewelry as Tahitian is extremely deceptive.

It's fairly easy to identify glass pearls because of their uniform size, shape, and color. Make sure you identify the component as glass and not pearl. Don't sniff at the fact they are glass. Glass pearls can make awesome pieces of jewelry. I fell in love with and bought a glass pearl choker with an elaborate ball clasp by designer Judith Leiber years ago. Discounted, the price was $450.

Gemstones

Few non-precious gemstones are untreated. Some examples can be amethyst, white topaz, and iolite. All the precious colored gemstones are usually treated in one way or another. It's not bad to use treated gemstones; everyone does. Just make sure you label your jewelry with the correct treatment.

Here is a guide to common gemstone treatments:

- Heating—brings about the desired alteration of color or clarity.
- Bleaching—the use of chemical agents to lighten or remove a gemstone's color.
- Waxing and oiling—using colorless wax, paraffin, and/or oil in porous opaque gemstones to improve their appearance.
- Lasering—the use of lasers and chemicals to alter inclusions in diamonds.
- Dyeing—using artificial means to give a gemstone new color, intensify present color, or improve to color uniformity.

At times, cost constraints will dictate that you use other than "real" gemstones. I just finished making a stunning bracelet using lab-created emeralds and imitation white faceted stones instead of diamonds. The difference in cost using lab-created materials was quite significant.

■ Imitation—This designation encompasses all man-made products such as glass, ceramic, or plastic designed to imitate or resemble the appearance, but not duplicate the characteristic properties, of a natural gemstone.

■ Lab-created—Grown in a lab instead of through nature, these gemstones have essentially the same optical, physical, and chemical properties as their naturally occurring counterparts.

Guides to Required Disclosures

The FTC Web site contains many links to important information affecting your jewelry making business. Find them by going to www.ftc.gov and doing a site search using the key phrase "jewelry enhancements."

The Nourish Your Spirit site contains a quick and easy guide to eighteen different gemstone enhancements and the abbreviations you use to indicate which enhancement is present. Find out more by going to www.nourish-your-spirit.com/ftc.html.

Lead

Many U.S. states do not allow jewelry makers to use any components containing lead in children's jewelry. If you use components containing lead, you must disclose this fact. You'll know if you are using lead components because your component supplier will make a similar disclosure.

The prior chapters in this book laid the groundwork for starting your home-based jewelry making business. The next chapter discusses how you can use successful marketing techniques to get your name and product out there, where your customer base awaits.

Now comes the fun part—making money by selling your jewelry! I devote all of chapter 11 to the subject of setting up a Web site and e-commerce. This chapter is all about marketing your jewelry in other venues. Some cost money and some do not.

Press Kits

Chapter 5 of this book discusses how to prepare a press release. A current press release is part of a press kit, which you update less frequently than a press release.

Do you ever wonder why certain shops in your local area always seem to be featured in the fashion section of your local newspaper? Well, it's probably because the shop owner makes it very easy for the editor of that section by providing current, relevant information about their business.

Let's face it: There are only so many hours in a day. The editor will greatly appreciate your killer press kit because it makes their job of providing readers with interesting, relevant copy that much easier.

Components of a Press Kit

Pitch Letter

This letter is tailored to the recipient and explains why you sent the press kit. Inherent to the pitch letter is how the recipient can use the press kit to increase their efficiency and effectiveness with their customer base.

Fact Sheet

This is an outline of what is contained in the press kit.

Artist Résumé

Include any facts in your résumé that assert your skill and knowledge level. Some suggestions: education, experience, juried shows you participated in, awards received, and how long you have been in business.

Product Information

Include what fabrication methods and materials you use. Tell a story about your jewelry. Maybe you have based your designs on beaded jewelry found in prehistoric graves, or maybe you use forging techniques dating back to the nineteenth century. Play up any and all unique angles.

Pictures

Include line sheets (more about these later in this chapter) and slides with high-resolution images.

Press Releases

Update your press kit when facts change. Update your press releases much more frequently.

Local Retail Shops

This is an excellent place to start, as you will easily be able to do all your homework prior to contacting the owner of the shop. In every midsized and up metropolitan area there is a part of the city that is known as a trendy arts district. Handcrafted jewelry fits into this shopping venue very well.

Look for retail shops selling unique clothing and household items. Maybe the owner of the shop is the designer of the items sold in the shop as well. This is a plus, as the owner already knows that customers appreciate and value handcrafted goods.

Could be that you're already a customer of some of these shops. Face recognition by the owner is a good starting point, but your knowledge of the types of items the owner likes to sell is even better. If it's a clothing store and the owner of the shop likes to sell Vivienne Tam or Nicole Miller garments, check out those designers' runway shows and print ads to see what style of jewelry they are showing with their garments.

It's a safe bet the buyer/owner for the shop is also familiar with the accessories shown with the garments. If you have ever owned a retail shop or worked on commission, you know it's all about the up-selling. Like the dress? Here's a scarf to match. If the designer isn't showing a lot of jewelry with the garments, grab your color wheel and plan out a colored gemstones scheme to go with the garments.

How to Use a Color Wheel

Due to our boxes of Crayola Crayons in grade school, most of us are familiar with the color terms *primary, secondary,* and *tertiary*. Color is very evocative. It is very important to understand the language of color when you mix colors in your jewelry, especially if you are designing jewelry for specific garments.

Primary colors are blue, red, and yellow. These are colors in their pure states— not combined with any other colors. *Secondary* colors are violet, orange, and green. These colors are a mixture of two primary colors.

- red and yellow = orange
- yellow and blue = green
- blue and red = purple

Tertiary colors are a mix of a *primary* color and a *secondary* color. For example, turquoise is a mixture of blue (primary color) and green (secondary color). *Complementary* colors are those that are opposite each other on a color wheel.

A complete color wheel, available at any arts and crafts store, will show the complementary color combination for many other secondary and tertiary colors. It is visually very striking to pair complementary colors. The key to pairing complementary colors is to make sure that one complementary color is dominant.

For example, a red dress paired with an emerald or green jade necklace is attractive, whereas a red top teamed with a green skirt, unless you are an elf, is unsightly. If two complementary colors are paired with equal strength, your eye does not know where to focus, thus creating an impression of disharmony.

Missing from the color wheel are all neutral colors: black, white, and brown. If you think about it, these three colors can be combined with any of the colors on the color wheel for a harmonious look.

How to Sell to Local Retail Shops

You have done your homework. You are familiar with the shop's target market, and your jewelry is a good fit. Your next job is to find out the name of the owner and figure out how often they are on-site. If you always carry business cards and a brochure with you, it's very natural to make a soft sales pitch while shopping.

It's always a good idea to have a battle plan prior to entering the store. You know they sell a really cool plum top. You design a peridot gemstone necklace to accessorize with the top. Wear the necklace into the shop, try on the top, and solicit an opinion from the salesperson helping you. You may luck out and have the owner assisting you. Somehow, slip it into the conversation that you are a jewelry designer and the necklace you are wearing is self-created.

A friend owns a chain of surf shops. A fairly regular customer who designs surf-related jewelry just flat-out asked if the owner would like to carry his line of jewelry while paying for a swimsuit. What clinched the deal was the fact that the jewelry designer had a small plastic display rack stocked with appropriate jewelry ready to go in his car. The jewelry designer had really done his homework, even going so far as selecting a spot in the shop where it was possible to place the rack.

By eliminating all potential challenges to placing his jewelry, the jewelry designer really made it hard for the shop owner to say no. His investment in a swimsuit and a few other purchases really paid off, as that designer's jewelry has been a strong seller in this chain of surf shops for many years.

Suppose just cold-calling the shop owner isn't your thing, and you just can't get up the gumption to make it your thing. The next-best option is to have a brochure and sample delivered to the owner. Follow up with a telephone call in a few days. If the owner has no interest at that time, ask if the owner is interested in receiving information about your jewelry designs in the future. If the answer is no, it's still not a bad idea to send the shop owner a yearly promotional brochure in September for the holiday season.

Selling on Consignment

Many retail shops and galleries just aren't willing to buy much work outright. While selling on consignment can be scary, it's a good way for a new jewelry artist to get their foot in the door.

Here is my list of consignment sale tips:

- Don't place items with a brand-new shop or gallery.
- Establish a time limit for the consignment relationship.
- A 50 percent commission is standard; make sure you have a meeting of the minds as to your commission.
- Establish terms for discounting the jewelry.
- Discuss who will bear the risk if a piece on consignment is stolen or damaged.
- If the jewelry is sterling silver, make sure the shop or gallery understands how to keep the jewelry tarnish-free.

In-Home Jewelry Shows

Some people love in-home shows, while others consider them a waste of time. If you have a friend with a wide base of friends who is willing to open their home for a show, this is a good way to test the waters. It also gives you an excellent chance to practice your sales skills in front of a somewhat-accepting audience.

When people attend in-home shows, they more or less have already decided they will make a purchase. It's somewhat awkward to attend a show, eat the refreshments, and walk out without buying something. So make sure you have a wide variety of jewelry, both in design and price.

Also, be prepared to have a question-and-answer session on the jewelry and a gift for your hostess. It's an excellent idea to describe the quality and origin of all the gemstones used in the jewelry. Also, give a thumbnail sketch of how you fabricate the jewelry. People love the terms *forged* and *hammered*. If you make your own clasps, be sure to emphasize that fact. It's not too hard to handcraft a hook-and-eye clasp, and it adds a lot to the unique nature of the piece of jewelry.

Local Museum Gift Shops

If you can put an ethnic or historical spin on your jewelry, museum gift shops are also a recommendation. All museums have permanent collections and temporary exhibits. Many museums publish their planned temporary exhibitions many months in advance. Use this information to tailor a line of jewelry to the specific exhibition.

For example, if a planned exhibit is African Textiles, create a line of jewelry capitalizing on the social use of beads in Africa. If an exhibit of Georgia O'Keeffe paintings is on the agenda, construct some jewelry based upon designs from the American Southwest.

One way to become familiar with the key players at the museum is to volunteer, or become a member to show your support. Failing that, pay a visit to the museum's gift shop to check out the price range of jewelry they already offer. You'll want to stay in line with these prices. While you are there, either speak with or get the name of the manager so you can make your pitch and drop off a brochure. At the very least, find out if the gift shop must follow any purchasing protocol. Based upon the answers you get to the above, you'll be able to come up with a plan of attack.

Most gift shops seem quite open to new product lines as long as they tie into the theme of the museum. Of course, you don't want to come up with an entire line of jewelry on speculation unless you feel you will have another venue in which to sell it if your sales pitch is unsuccessful. Make sure you always have an alternative retail avenue.

Remember the Rhino software discussed in chapter 3? This is a perfect application of that (or similar) software. Use it to design a virtual line of jewelry tailored to the spec project. If your proposal is not accepted, the images can be modified for future projects, and you haven't laid out the time or money to create the actual designs.

Cooperative Craft Shows

Start by networking with other artists in your area. Ideally, six months before a holiday season, you should pull together a group of local artists and rent a location in which to have a cooperative arts and crafts show. Aim for a wide mix of specialties in addition to jewelry, from fiber to pottery to furniture. The wider your array of products, the more interest you will have for the show.

Protect yourself by getting nonrefundable deposits from each artist interested in participating in the show. I recommend a deposit of half the total cost early in the game. You'll need cash to give the owners of the craft show location a deposit, but equally as important, paying a deposit indicates serious interest on the part of your participants. A couple of weeks prior to the show, solicit payment in full.

Use every possible type of media to get the word out about your show. Hang posters in local shops, send out press kits, and arrange for some paid advertising. It's pretty easy to get free advertising for these types of shows. Contact the Lifestyle (or your newspaper's equivalent) editor and ask how far in advance they like to receive press releases for inclusion in the newspaper. Abide by their schedule and send a press release with full details about the show at the appropriate time. Include contact information and the fact that high-res jpegs are available, and the chances are good you will get a response. At the very least, solicit inclusion in the "What's Happening This Week" section of your local newspaper.

Contact all the free-to-the-public magazines and newspapers in your area. Inquire about the possibility of an article being written about your show. Whether or not this pans out, check on their advertising rates and take out a display ad a couple of weeks before—as well as during the week of—the show. Make sure you emphasize the fact that free parking is available (if this is indeed the case).

Should you charge *de minimis* admission to the show? This is a hard question to answer. Obviously, you are building in value for the show by charging an admission. Do some research to see what the standard is in your area. You could always offer free admission if the attendee brings in your magazine advertisement. This will also give you some valuable feedback as to the best places to advertise for future shows.

Another idea is to advertise that the admission fee benefits a local charity. Just remember that if you charge admission, you'll also have to hire someone to collect the money.

A good way to build some local name recognition is to give free demonstrations at related consumer shows. Check with your local convention center for their show schedule, and get in touch with the organizers of fashion-related shows.

Contact your local arts and crafts stores to see if they'd like to have you provide a jewelry making demonstration using a product they sell. Another possibility is your local library. I have attended many free demonstrations at my library, from a painting lesson given by a famous television quick painter to origami and organic gardening.

Free demonstrations will not do you a bit of good if you have no contact information to hand out to attendees. A Web site is the perfect way to consolidate all of your business facts. If you are not interested in e-commerce, every business should at least have an informational Web site that can be accessed by potential customers to find out how to purchase your jewelry. Find out more about making the Internet work for your business in the next chapter.

Donating Jewelry for Charitable Events and Fund-Raisers

An altruistic way to get your name in the public eye is to donate your product for charitable causes. Many charitable events have silent auctions. The organizers of the event will be delighted to include a well-made piece of jewelry.

Not to seem crass, but this is also an excellent way to get rid of discontinued items of jewelry. Just make sure you are proud of any piece you donate. After all, you want your name to be associated with quality work.

Call for Entries: Local Arts and Crafts Shows

If I applied to enter every arts and crafts show within driving distance, I would be a very busy woman. The possibilities for exposure and bringing in revenue are limitless. However, answering a call for entry is quite a bit different than sponsoring your own craft show. As they are normally juried, just because you apply and have the booth fee doesn't mean participation is a done deal.

Each show has criteria for entry. Make sure you read the application guidelines and provide all requested information in exactly the format required. A couple of obstacles that are easy to avoid: Make sure jewelry is indeed one of the show categories, and make sure you submit your application by the deadline.

The quality of your jewelry images is a key part of acceptance. It doesn't make any difference how stellar your jewelry is; if your images appear amateurish or digitally manipulated, your application will not be accepted. Carefully consider the pixel size, both maximum and minimum. For example, the specifications may state that images must be sized to at least 1,400 pixels but no greater than 2,000 pixels.

Most shows will also ask for an image of your booth setup. This is kind of a catch-22 situation. If you have never entered and been accepted into a juried show, you probably won't have a booth image. In that case, set up a mock booth in your garage or backyard. Crop the image so only your booth appears. It's a nice touch to have someone else take the picture so you are standing in the booth. You can also just take the photo yourself, using a tripod and your camera's timer.

Two important points of clarification for you as the artist to consider: expected attendance and security. Every show should have expected attendance available as part of the call for entry. This figure is based upon past attendance and is normally very accurate.

If the event is held outside, security is a major concern, as you won't want to break down and set up your booth each day. Regardless of security, I always transport all expensive jewelry items home with me each evening.

Why Didn't My Jewelry Sell?

There is nothing more disappointing than walking away from a show not even having covered your entry fee. Do a postmortem after each show to figure out what went wrong and what worked.

Price Points and Options

Maybe sales were down because your products didn't cover enough price points. It could be that you did not offer the right choice of jewelry. Some shows can tolerate pieces in the over-$100 price range, while others need to have a wide selection of options in the under-$30 range. If you plan properly, you can make as much money selling a $25 item as you do a $100 item. You might feel as if you are "piece-mealing" it, but what truly matters at the end of the day is what's in your cash box.

Customer Relations

How did you treat the customers who approached your booth? You'll guarantee yourself a poor sales day if you were reading a book or eating a snack while potential customers were showing some interest in your work. On the flip side, it's the kiss of death to stand by the entrance of your booth looking too desperate. I have found making simple pieces of jewelry while attending to your booth is a fantastic way to steady your nerves and be approachable at the same time.

If a customer enters your booth, smile and invite them to look at the work in progress. Show them the tools you use. Compliment the color of their outfit and give color choices that work well with the garment. A sleeveless top cries out for bangle bracelets; brown looks best with gold-toned jewelry; a choker looks fantastic on a long, slender neck—you get the idea. Pretty soon you are having a conversation that you both enjoy while you're increasing the chances that a sale will come to fruition.

Offer Options to Pay

Cash and Checks

Make sure you have options for paying. We all love to receive cash because the risk of collection is reduced to almost zero. Make sure you come prepared to make change. Most show presenters take checks with proper identification. Protect yourself by asking to see a driver's license. Make sure the name on the license matches the check and the picture on the license is indeed the person standing before you.

Write the driver's license number, date of birth, and telephone number on the face of the check. If your bank returns the check, use the information to contact the customer. Most people are inherently honest, are truly embarrassed if their check bounces, and will make good on it immediately. For the small percentage that is not, well, karma is the great equalizer.

Credit Cards

I covered this is in chapter 5, Getting Started. With Wi-Fi access, verifying credit cards is a snap. If the venue doesn't offer Wi-Fi, some high-speed Internet providers now offer mobile routers that bring wireless Internet to you. To use this system, simply insert a PC laptop card provided by a cellular carrier like Verizon, Sprint, or AT&T. The card provides the Internet connection while a mobile router completes the transaction. For more information about this, do a Google search using the key phrase "wi-fi to go."

Layaway

You can also offer extended payment terms. Take a nonrefundable deposit equal to your hard costs for the jewelry and add the cost of shipping the jewelry to the customer to the final price. Set a deadline for payment in full. If the customer does not complete the sale, at least you've covered the cost of materials.

Different Colors and Sizes

Not everyone loves the color green, or blue, or yellow. Seven and a half inches is the standard bracelet length in the United States, but remember—some people have smaller wrists and some, larger. While pierced ears are common, make sure you also have the tools with you to convert a pierced earring to a clip-on. Have a supply of necklace extenders available at the show as well.

Expand Outside Your Local Area

Using the same call-for-entry information as for national shows, attend regional shows as well. Most craft magazines have a section in the back of the magazine giving craft show information state by state. For example, you can't open a copy of *Metalsmith* magazine without seeing numerous calls for entry.

Investigate the entry criteria for those within easy driving distance, compare the booth fee to the expected attendance, and apply. Don't be discouraged if your first few entries are denied. Just keep honing your skills and remember what I said earlier in this book about the wow factor that is needed for juried events.

Once you have experience in your regional area, also consider national shows. If I could apply to and attend only one show a year, I would pick the Smithsonian Craft Show.

Smithsonian Craft Show

This show is held at the National Building Museum in Washington, D.C., each year for three days in the spring. This is one of the most prestigious shows in the United States. Advertising is massive, both local and national, which is reflected in the attendance numbers. They have a silent auction, which is a good way to get more exposure for your name and designs. They even have a first-time exhibitor award.

The Smithsonian Craft Show is geared toward one-of-a-kind, handcrafted pieces of jewelry. An overnight lockup is available for jewelers at a nominal fee. Booth fees are quite high, ranging upward to $2,000 and higher. You can find out more information about this show and get a glance at past shows on the Web site (www .smithsoniancraftshow.org).

A bonus is the fact that jewelry and wearable artists who were previously juried into the Smithsonian Craft Show have a chance to have their designs included in the Smithsonian Trunk Show. Also held at the National Building Museum in Washington, D.C., this show takes place in late September, making it a more suitable venue for holiday shopping.

American Craft Retailers Expo (ACRE)

Juried as well, consider this show if you sell wholesale. Taking place in the spring of each year in Las Vegas, Nevada, it boasts 1,600 registered retailers. ACRE is tied in with wholesalecrafts.com, an online marketplace matching wholesale providers with interested sellers.

Unlike other shows where totally handcrafted is the key, wholesale events such as this only require original design and some handcrafting—not difficult criteria to meet, as even production-line jewelry is manipulated by real people during the process. Bead artists must have five prior wholesale accounts in order to apply (up from two in the past).

ACRE offers three payment plans for the booth fees, which approximate those charged by the Smithsonian Craft Show. If you're interested in selling wholesale, this is a fantastic place to start. Find out more about this wholesale show at www .acrelasvegas.com.

National Exposure

Cooperative National Print Ads

Just as you can network with other artists to hold your own craft show, you can also form a nationwide cooperative comprised of many independent designers working in various mediums. After you've formed a cooperative, do your research and see which national magazines attract your members' overall demographic.

Next, query possible magazines as to their advertising rate for a full-page advertisement. Solicit interest from your cooperative membership. The price of the ad will fluctuate depending on the number of participants. Find out the specifications for submission to the magazine and have an experienced member of your cooperative lay out the ad copy.

I was a member of a cooperative a few years back that has subsequently disbanded. Placing a national ad is much easier than it sounds if you divide the tasks among your members. Space in the potential ads was publicized to the members about three months prior to the newsstand release date (this will vary based upon the publication). Payment in full was collected immediately via the cooperative's PayPal account.

It was a positive experience for me revenue-wise. I eventually dropped out because it was apparent the original organizers of the cooperative were dealing with some members in a prejudicial fashion.

Getting Your Jewelry on Television Shows and in Gift Bags

Designers constantly attempt to capitalize on the popularity of a celebrity, television show, or motion picture to push their products. At many advertising agencies, there are whole departments devoted to placing products in shows.

For those that don't want to pay the high advertising agency fees, getting your jewelry worn by celebrities or by actors on television shows is no different in theory from any other marketing effort. You need to find out who the contact person is for the celebrity or show, put together a modified press kit, enclose a sample, and mail out the package.

The Lookbook

A fantastic resource for the fashion industry and stylists is The Lookbook. Set up an account at www.thelookbook.com, and you'll be able to search their database to see what stylists handle which celebrities, or vice versa.

For example, do you think you have the perfect necklace for Jennifer Hudson? Per The Lookbook, her stylist is Jessica Paster. The Lookbook provides the address, telephone number, and e-mail address so you can make contact.

Do a cost-benefit analysis. You are not going to get the sample back. More than likely, one of the office staff will end up wearing it. Additionally, do television shows or celebrities actually pay for items worn for business? Well, some do. Angelina Jolie was given a pair of Lana Jewelry La Bangles 14K gold hoop earrings by the designer to wear to the premiere of *Mr. and Mrs. Jones*. She liked them so much she purchased them for her personal use.

However, if you are not being paid for your work, will the cachet of having your jewelry placed on a television show equate to cold hard cash? That's right, you're a business person. If it's not going to make you money, is it worth the effort?

The last time I checked, the cost of placing an item in a major event swag bag was $40,000. That's right—$40,000, on top of the cost of making the jewelry and getting it to the event sponsor. I see no advantageous cost-benefit in this equation for the home-based jewelry maker. For $40,000 you can enter twenty Smithsonian Craft Shows and probably make at least twice your booth cost.

Agency Placement

To get more information on placing your jewelry on television shows or in gift bags, check out Luxe MG's Web site at www.luxemg.com. They have provided gift bags for Lindsay Lohan, Carrie Underwood, and the Grammy Awards, and have provided products worn by contestants on *The Bachelor* television show on ABC.

11

How to Make the Internet and e-Commerce Work for Your Business

Even if you don't want to sell your jewelry online, a Web site is a fantastic way to provide your customers with more information about your company. Web sites aren't all that difficult to maintain yourself if you are so inclined. Hosting—a big expense in the past—is now very inexpensive.

Establishing Your Own Web Site

Web Site in a Box

I am a big proponent of building your own Web site if you have the time and basic HTML knowledge. Most do-it-yourself Web-site builders have a wizard to walk you through the steps, using toolbars and text editors that are very similar to those used in word processing programs. Here are the basic steps:

- Choose a template from the available selection
- Customize the template with color, font, and style
- Add your own copy
- Upload images
- Publish

It's pretty easy. You could have a bare-bones Web site done and published within an hour. Many do-it-yourself Web-site builders also allow for modifications, such as uploading pages you create using Microsoft Office FrontPage or Dreamweaver and plugging in your own HTML coding in certain fields to customize the look.

Web.com

I've been a happy customer of this do-it-yourself service for many years. The wizard is easy to use, customer support is usually readily available, and I can remember few instances over the years where my site was down because of problems at Web.com.

Hosting and the monthly service fee are very inexpensive. My only complaint is the home-page templates do look like obvious templates (in my opinion, not very professional-looking). However, Web.com has a staff of developers who can customize any aspect of your site for you—at an additional charge, of course.

Yahoo Stores

I've never had a Yahoo store. Friends that do report it is very similar in nature to other do-it-yourself Web-site services. After viewing the demo, I agree with their opinion.

eBay Stores

eBay also offers the same type of service as Yahoo.

Using a Web-Site Design Company

Another more-costly option is to hire a designer to create a Web site especially for you. This can cost tens of thousands of dollars or more. Keep in mind as well that every time you want to modify your site, it's going to cost you additional service fees.

How to Format Simple HTML Commands

HyperText Markup Language (HTML) is a popular markup language used to create Web pages. Web pages are created using a text file such as Notepad if you are using Windows, or SimpleText if you are a Mac user. You can also use the two software applications I spoke about earlier in this chapter, FrontPage or Dreamweaver.

There are three facts to remember when creating a Web page using HTML:

1. Always use the lowercase for your HMTL code.
2. Your text files are saved with an HTML extension (.html).
3. Most HTML tags have an opening tag and a closing tag: <p> is an example of an opening tag and </p> is an example of a closing tag.

For an excellent (and free) online HTML tutorial, visit www.quackit.com/html. You will be able to find out how to code just about any tag you need to create a Web page. If you plan to use a do-it-yourself Web-site builder, knowing some simple HTML tags will help you further customize the available templates.

Honestly, I think your start-up money is better spent on advertising and creating professional press kits. If you decide that hiring a Web-site design company is an option for you, here are some tips to follow when selecting one:

- View some of their prior work directly as uploaded to the Internet.
- Ask for and call references.
- Are they a one-stop shop offering hosting, search-engine marketing, and other Web-related services?
- Will they give you a written proposal and firm deadline?
- Will you be able to view the work in progress and make modifications to the design as it's built?

Consistency

Whether you do it yourself or use a design company, it is important that your Web site have a consistent feel among all its pages. Color schemes, types of graphics, fonts, and page layouts should be the same on each of your Web pages.

By repeating these key elements, you give your site a consistent feel that creates and then reinforces your company's distinct identity. In addition, consistency allows your readers to adapt quickly to your design and to confidently predict the location of information and navigation controls across all of your site pages.

Informational-Only Web Sites

Your informational Web site should contain the following pages that are linked and accessible from your home page:

Company Information

This is where you provide your company overview. Discuss your design philosophy, any special jewelry training or education, the materials and techniques you use, and some personalized information telling how you happened to open a jewelry making business.

Collection

Even though you don't want to participate in e-commerce, it's important to have your entire jewelry collection available for viewing on your Web site. It comes in handy when you want to present your collection to any potential big accounts to which you can wholesale. Also, combined with a where-to-buy link, individuals can see your jewelry and visit retail shops for purchase.

Where to Buy

List all stores carrying your jewelry with complete address and contact information. If no stores currently carry your jewelry, skip this link until you have a couple of shops to list.

Company News

List anything new going on with your business. This is a great place to list arts and crafts shows you will be attending. Potential customers who have skimmed through your online collection and have an interest in purchasing will know when you'll be in their area. I've had customers e-mail me to see if I could bring a certain piece of jewelry to the show. If you've won any awards or been accepted into juried competitions, make sure you include this information as well.

Press

List any magazines or newspapers that have featured your jewelry. Get an image of the magazine cover and specific page in the magazine from the publisher, or take the picture yourself and upload it to this page. You might also include links to these articles if they are available in an electronic version.

Believe me, the circulation of high-quality press kits and press releases combined with stellar pieces of jewelry will have you featured in the press in a relatively short period of time. At the very least, hound your local newspaper's style editor until you are featured in that venue.

Links

I'll talk more about links and search-engine ranking later in this chapter. For now, just keep in mind that this page is where you list your links with other complementary Web sites.

Blogs

A blog is comparable to an online diary. It's a place for you to quickly jot down any business news and give your customers a look at what's going on in your day-to-day life as a jewelry artist. Your entries should be fairly regular and are commonly displayed in reverse-chronological order.

Contact Information

I highly recommend that you do *not* list your home address. I do list my business telephone number and e-mail address. You can also use this page to invite those interested to sign up for your mailing list.

e-Commerce Web Sites

An e-commerce Web site has all of the above, with the added capability of allowing viewers to make purchases from your Web site.

Getting Paid

PayPal

PayPal has been the king of online payment processing for the past ten years. I think the PayPal system works very efficiently and effectively. With PayPal, your business doesn't need a merchant account. PayPal acts as your credit card processor! If you want or need a merchant account, you can set this up with PayPal also.

How PayPal Works

Use your e-mail address to set up a PayPal account into which you transfer money. Then use this account to purchase items online, pay bills, or accept payments from customers who don't wish to share their credit card information with your business.

It's a pretty stress-free way of doing business for the seller. Even better, if you ship items to a PayPal-confirmed address using some sort of delivery confirmation, you'll most likely have protection from charge-backs due to customer disputes. PayPal has a great seller's protection plan!

Other Payment Processors

If you would like to check out the services of payment providers other than PayPal, here are a few possibilities. Find out more about each by doing a Google search using the name as your keyword. Make sure you understand the services provided by each payment processor and their fees prior to making a commitment:

- WorldPay
- Paynet Systems
- 2Checkout
- ChronoPay
- CCNow

If you sell goods or services through your Web site, you must have a policies page. It's just good business to advise your customers on the terms and conditions of their purchase. You'll also cut down on the amount of e-mail you'll have to respond to regarding returns and shipping.

Images for the Web

Taking pictures for your Web site is a unique art totally unlike shooting images for print ads, brochures, or press kits. When you produce a brochure, everyone who looks at it is looking at the exact same image printed on the exact same paper. When you upload images to the Internet, your viewers will be looking at the images using different Web browsers and varying degrees of screen resolution. Another problem you must deal with is sizing the images for quick rendering.

Web Browsers

You should test your Web site in different browsers to make sure your pages are rendering as close as possible to the way you want them to appear. Unless you have a bunch of different computers, there is no way you can possibly do this yourself.

Sample Policies Page

Payment Processing

Maire Loughran accepts the following forms of payment:

- MasterCard
- VISA
- American Express
- Discover
- PayPal

We do not accept payment by check or money order. We do not send orders COD. All payments are processed through our shopping cart using state-of-the-art SSL encryption.

Luckily, there are free open-source online services staffed by volunteers who will do the testing for you. The service will ask questions regarding browsers, screen size, and color depth. Input your testing preferences and between fifteen minutes to just over an hour later, you will have screenshots of your site as displayed per your testing specifications.

View your screenshots, and if your site looks less than perfect when viewed using a particular browser, it's time to see how many of your visitors access your site using that browser. Let's say your home page columns look funny when viewed using Internet Explorer 6. Depending on the number of visitors you have using Internet Explorer 6, this may not be high on your priority level to fix.

Web Browser Testing

The leader in free web browser testing services is Browsershots (browsershots.org). The home page has an online interview with options for you to check off. Enter your Web-site address and submit. You can check the process using the site's *Queue* option. When your job is finished, the results will come up in the site's *Screenshots* menu option.

Checking Visitor Stats

You should be doing this task often for marketing purposes. You can get a wealth of information, such as what was your most frequent entry page, and the average time viewers spent visiting your Web site. You'll also be able to see your site's referring browsers, operating systems, and search engines.

Web-site analytics service comes as part of the package with many do-it-yourself Web-site builders. You can also use Google's free analytics program (www.google.com/analytics). You have to remember that not all of your viewers will have upgraded to the most current browser. Check the percentage of visitors who access your site using a browser with iffy presentation. If the percentage is not high, this may be an issue you can ignore.

Shooting images for your Web site is quite different from images for print, a topic covered in chapter 10. Most point-and-shoot digital cameras automatically save at a file resolution of 72 ppi (pixels per inch). The good news is that this is the best resolution for viewing your images on a computer monitor.

Troubleshooting Digital Images

The fact that your images must look flawless just can't be emphasized enough. If your Web site has e-commerce capabilities, a stellar picture goes a long way toward reinforcing customer confidence in your product. This translates into sales. If your site is for informational purposes only, you still need great images to attract customers to your shows.

Automation Is Bad

Turn off your camera's auto-select option. This option controls many aspects of taking pictures that are appropriate for shooting on a sunny day outdoors. The problem is that you're shooting jewelry in a studio. You need to play around with your camera's features to get the best effect.

Exposure

If your images are too light or too dark, the solution is to use your camera's exposure control. My digital camera is automatically set at 1, with varying steps in exposure from -2 to +2. I have found that most of my jewelry images look better shot anywhere from +1 to +2. To cover all the bases, I normally shoot a few images set at each exposure level between that range.

Color

This is no longer so much of an issue for me because of my Ortery Photosimile Light Box, but different lighting causes different color casts to your image. This is most obvious when you shoot your jewelry on a dead-white background and the image appears to be on a light blue background. This is very unprofessional-looking.

Correct this by using your camera's white balance control. Use your normal shooting lights to take a picture of a white paper or poster board. View the image on your monitor; if it looks completely white, you have a winner. Save that setting and use it to shoot the rest of your photos. If it's still slightly blue or gray, play around with your camera's settings until your white balance setting is shooting with a white background.

Blurry Images

Since you have turned off your camera's auto feature, unless you use a tripod, your images will be blurry. Tripods are inexpensive; invest in one if you don't already own one.

Backgrounds

Try to avoid shooting with a gray-colored background; it never adds anything to your image. This is another reason why it's so important to get your white balance under control. For more information on backdrops, refer to chapter 3.

Lighting

A good rule of thumb is to use hard light for soft surfaces and soft light for hard surfaces. Most jewelry fits in the hard-surface category. Your camera's electronic flash produces hard light; so does a single spotlight focused on the work. There are various methods to produce soft light.

Here is a thumbnail sketch of the different options you can use. Keep in mind that you may obtain the best image of your jewelry by combining options. The key is experimentation.

- Photo umbrellas
- Floodlights
- Attaching foam-core board or a LumiQuest Soft Screen to your camera's flash
- Softbox
- Light tents
- Black or white board placed in a light tent to further bounce light
- Reflective risers

Screen Resolution

Those accessing the Internet most commonly use a resolution of 1024 x 768 pixels. I prefer another resolution, but to make my life easier, I've reset the screen resolution on the computer I use for image editing and uploading to the norm of 1024 x 768.

Quick Rendering of Images

Stop right now and think about the amount of patience you have while waiting for a Web page to render. Back in the day, before the proliferation of high-speed Internet, that is why many sites had splash pages. The point was to have a fast-loading intro page to keep the viewer interested while the rest of the site rendered behind it.

Splash pages are a bit of an anachronism now, but the concept is still the same. You can't count on the fact that your viewer is using anything but dial-up. If it takes too long for your image to render, many viewers will close out of the site. I suggest using thumbnail sizes of your images while giving your viewer the ability to click on the thumbnail for a larger view.

Splash Pages

A splash page is the introductory page into your site. As it loads, the rest of your site will load behind it. You'll know you're on a splash page because there will be an *Enter, Skip,* or similar command button to move you out of the splash into the substance of the site. I still see them occasionally in use. I find them annoying; I am not alone. Some studies shows 25 percent of viewers don't stick around to get past the splash page.

Search Engine Optimization (SEO)

If you have a fantastic Web site, it will do you no good unless people can find it. It's kind of like a needle in a haystack out there in cyberspace. Increase your chances of potential customers finding you through search engine optimization.

To understand how this works, think about how you would find a vendor for aquamarine faceted gemstones on the Internet. You would type the key phrase "aquamarine faceted gemstones" in your favorite search engine. The pages that result from your search are listed in order of their ranking with the search engine. How far do you scroll through the list? The first page? The second? Internet statistics reveal that most visitors only scroll through the first twenty listings. Being ranked in the first ten listings for your keywords and phrases is excellent.

Select Keywords/Phrases

When you write pages for your Web site, identify words and phrases that describe the particular subject of the page. To be the most effective, these words and phrases should be succinct and precise. Each key phrase should have no more than five words. Think about this as a customer would. What keywords would you use if you wanted to find your style of jewelry on the Internet?

You also don't want the keywords to be too generic. At the time I wrote this book, I used the keyword "aquamarine" as a Google search. The first ten hits didn't even have anything to do with the gemstone; rather, they pertained to a children's movie. When I modified my search to the key phrase "aquamarine faceted gemstones," I found suitable vendors.

Use the Keywords Often

Your home page should be an overall description of your site with an array of links (usually located on a toolbar that runs horizontally across the top of the home page, or vertically on the left side of the home page) leading to subsidiary pages within your site. These pages can further link on and on to many different pages.

Once you've identified your keywords, use them in the title of your Web pages. Repeat the keywords frequently throughout the text on each page. Search engines view each of your pages, looking for good relevant keywords that are naturally integrated within the material on the page.

Gone are the days of keyword stacking. This involved just repeating the keywords repeatedly, usually in type color that was not visible to the viewer. Don't do it. You will only accomplish getting your site banned by the search engines. Make sure to use your keywords naturally throughout the text.

Organizing the Page

Each page should contain between 400 to 600 words. Don't have a jumbled mess of unorganized, run-on paragraphs. Each paragraph should be between three to five sentences. Break paragraphs up with bold headings and subheads. Use your keywords in the headings. If appropriate, throw in ordered and numbered lists to further break up the text, making it easier for your visitor to read.

Backing into Your Keywords

Rather than choosing keywords and using them naturally within a page, you can also cherry-pick popular relevant keywords and design a page around those keywords. Obviously, for the keyword to be effective, it does have to pertain to the subject of jewelry. Tailoring a page around the keywords "galvanic corrosion" may bring many visitors to your site. However, not many of them will stick around to buy your jewelry.

Google has a fantastic tool for selecting keywords. The web address for this tool is https://adwords.google.com/select/KeywordToolExternal. You can also find it by doing a Google search with the key phrase "adword keyword tool." Just type your proposed keywords into the text box and Google will bring up both the competition for the keywords and the search volume.

Start a Content Web

Search engines aren't in the business of altruistically providing information. They want to keep viewers coming back to use their services because doing so provides the search engine's source of revenue. In order to keep their visitors coming back, they want to provide the most relevant information available for the requested keywords.

A good way to increase the search engine's reliance on the information you provide is by using a content web technique. Here's how a content web works:

- You write a page relevant to your site, rich with very precise niche keywords that brings your page up in the first ten search listings.
- Use inbound and outbound links to different complementary pages in your site.
- Don't overwhelm your reader. Limit links to three to five per page.
- Your niche keyword page will serve to drive traffic to other relevant pages within your site that may not be as highly ranked due to the popularity of the keywords.

- The more engaged your visitor is with your site, the higher the probability they will make the decision to buy.
- Search engines "see" your numerous linked pages with good relevant text. Ranking on other pages will start to improve.

Don't confuse content webs with link farms. Using link farms is a form of black hat marketing that can get you kicked out of search engine indexes. A link farm is a group of Web sites that link inbound between themselves in an artificial attempt to increase ranking. There's no attempt to provide good relevant content to the viewers.

Google's webmaster's section outlines some of the illicit practices that may lead to a site being removed entirely from the Google index or otherwise penalized. You can find this highly informative page by doing a Google search using the key phrase "webmaster tools."

Google Sitemap

Google has been the search engine leader for many years. To make it easier for Google to crawl through your site, consider preparing a sitemap. A Google Sitemap is a list of the pages on your Web site. Creating and submitting a Sitemap helps ensure that Google knows about all the pages on your site. This is particularly helpful if your site is new and doesn't have many inbound links.

Google put Sitemap into BETA test mode in 2006. I'm not exactly a computer-programming wizard, but I was able to create and upload a Sitemap to my Web.com e-commerce site with little fuss. I definitely recommend it for all new and existing sites—especially those with few inbound links.

Google's very helpful webmaster section covers Sitemaps and many other relevant topics, such as submitting your site to Google, promoting your site with Google Adwords, and how to find out if your site is being indexed.

Social Networking

Unless you live in a cave, you've probably heard about Facebook and MySpace. Both are Web sites that you use to identify your interests and upload images, post blogs, and communicate with other like-minded members.

I think you'll find opinion equally divided on this issue. Some business owners love social networking and find it a great way to get their name out there. Some think it's too much work for little reward.

An excellent discussion on how to use social networking is in the Webtrends section of about.com. Find it at webtrends.about.com. On the left-hand toolbar under *Browse Topic,* select *Social Networking.*

Blogging Tools

Your do-it-yourself Web-site builder package or designer can easily set up a blog within your site. It's a good place to add contemporaneous information about new products, shows, or sales. If you take the time to update a blog, make sure you also ping it.

If your Web site doesn't have a blog tool, or you haven't yet set up a Web site, you can use free blogger tools such as WordPress and Blogger. Both can be accessed by doing a Google search using those keywords. Some blogger sites have certain rights over your images once they are uploaded. Always read the fine print and make sure you are happy with the terms of your agreement with the blogging tool.

SEO is an art requiring constant care. You can be completely happy with your keyword rankings one day, and the next find that you've fallen below the top twenty listings because the search engine changed its ranking algorithm or some other odd event has transpired.

If a page is ranking well, it's always best not to fool around with it until its ranking decreases. Also, use careful consideration before paying any company that guarantees to increase your search engine ranking for a fee.

Pinging is the electronic equivalent of knocking on someone's door and handing them your blog entry. In this case, you are telling the Weblog tracking sites that you have updated your site.

Some suggestions on where to go to ping:

Technorati—http://technorati.com/ping
Weblogs.com—http://rpc.weblogs.com
Blo.gs.com—http://blo.gs/ping.php

Shopping Cart Software

Anyone accepting credit cards needs to coordinate their payment system with shopping cart software. It's very important to check with your merchant account provider to see which shopping cart software is compatible with their system.

If you plan to use PayPal's Website Payments Pro, they have a capability link accessible from their Website Payments overview page, showing more than seventy-five different carts that are pre-integrated to work with PayPal. Any other merchant account system you may be working with will be able to provide you with the same information.

Using a Web-site designer to custom-build your site? They will be able to pick up all the info they need regarding HTML variables supported for use with the Buy Now, Add to Cart, and View Cart buttons you'll need, as well as HTML variables supporting the Cart Upload command from your merchant account provider.

Setting Up Your Shopping Cart

I use a pre-integrated shopping cart with my PayPal merchant account that I set up myself. Following the shopping cart provider's instructions exactly, it's a fairly stress-free procedure. Most will run you through a wizard asking questions about shipping, sales tax, and other information related to the sales transaction.

You'll be provided with some basic code that you'll customize, based on your item's name and sales price. Once you get the basics down, it doesn't take but a second to create new product listings. The reason I like handling this myself is that with a click of the mouse, I can instantly change the price of my product instead of waiting for a programmer to add it to their queue of jobs.

Secure Sockets Layer (SSL)

Part of your responsibility to your customers is to keep their personal data private. Make sure your shopping cart provider has SSL capability. SSL encrypts data, like credit card numbers (as well as other personally identifiable information), which prevents hackers from stealing your customers' information and using it to fund their vacation in Belize.

You know that you are on an SSL-protected page when the address begins with "https" or there is a padlock icon at the bottom of the page. The lock icon is not just a picture. Click (or double-click) on it to see details of the site's security. For more information about this very important facet of e-commerce, visit www.ssl.com.

Sample Shopping Cart with HTML Code and SSL

For an excellent example of a shopping cart, check out www.milanjewelry.com. On the left-hand toolbar, click *Bella > Marianna Necklace*.

The drop-down selections for color are examples of select lists. The *Add to Bag* and *Submit* buttons are examples of action commands. Both are easy to format using the HTML code discussed in this chapter. Most do-it-yourself Web-site software will allow for this programming as well.

If you add an item to your shopping cart and view it, you'll notice changes: The Web address changes to https and the shopping cart page has a lock indicating you have SSL protection before entering your personal information.

Third-Party Marketing

Maybe setting up a Web site just isn't for you. There are third-party marketing sites through which you can sell your jewelry. Many jewelry artists also use third-party sites to complement their own Web site. For example, you can sell your lower-priced products on Etsy while your own site reflects your top-of-the-line designer pieces.

Etsy.com

To get started selling your jewelry on Etsy, all you need to do is register by picking out a unique identifier for your Etsy store and a password. Registration is free. Etsy charges twenty cents to list an item for four months. When the item sells, you owe Etsy a 3.5 percent commission. If you don't renew your listing fee after four months, your items drop from the site. There is no long-term contract or difficulty in extricating yourself or your shop from this site.

There are a few requirements to sell your jewelry on Etsy. The jewelry must be handmade by you. It can't be a knock-off of another designer's work. You are also not allowed to sell mass-produced work.

Etsy also has a section to sell supplies. So, if you got a shipment of ruby and only used half of it, you can list the other half for purchase by other designers. If you open an Etsy store, I also suggest you create simple jewelry making kits to sell in this section.

RubyLane.com

Ruby Lane has a slightly more strict application process. Anyone can start a shop, but the shop is subject to a rigorous inspection process prior to its going live on the site. You must have at least ten items in your shop at all times.

I experimented with opening a Ruby Lane shop while doing research for this book and found it to be a very organized and efficient system. They have warning systems in place that will tell you if your description for an item is potentially not in accordance with the FTC rules I discussed earlier in this book. This especially pertains to items with descriptions containing the terms *pearl*, *silver*, and *gold*. There is also an item-description spell check in place, something that I find helpful for a professional presentation.

Costs to open and maintain a shop are reasonable. The $75 setup fee is waived if your shop is not approved. After that, a $35 monthly charge covers both your shop and advertising. If you decide to close your shop, there is a *Close Shop* option on the Shop Owners home page that accomplishes that task with no fuss.

My shop was open for four months, and during that time I sold two pieces of jewelry. I'm not sure whether or not this is typical, as I only kept ten pieces of jewelry in my shop. To get a better idea of potential earnings, each shop has a crown rating indicating items sold and how long the shop has been in operation. Many of Ruby Lane's artisan jewelry shops have been open for more than four years. I would imagine this indicates a reasonable cost-benefit relationship.

ArtfulHome.com

Recently renamed from The Guild, the Artful Home Web site is a juried marketplace for many different types of artists. You set the wholesale price; Artful Home sets the retail. One of their jurors is Michael Monroe, who acted as curator and director of the Renwick Gallery of the Smithsonian Institution for twenty-one years. Get accepted at Artful Home and you should be able to pass muster for the Smithsonian Craft Show as well.

Six to ten high-res images at 300 ppi are required for the jury process. It is extremely critical that your images be stellar. If you are serious about your application and can't take great images, hire a professional jewelry photographer.

There is a $35 nonrefundable processing fee. The jury process normally takes two months from start to finish. Before applying, check out a few of the jewelry artist pages to see the quality of image you will need and examples of artist statements.

Other Online Catalogs

It is extremely difficult to get your jewelry included in other online catalogs such as Robert Redford's Sundance.com or Novica.com. If the site has a submission or new artist link, check out their guidelines for submission and follow the instructions exactly.

For example, to get placed in the Sundance catalog, they request that you send photos of your product and pricing information to their Merchandising Department Product Submission, Sundance Catalog, 3865 West 2400 South, Salt Lake City, Utah, 84120, or via e-mail at samplesubmission@sundance.net.

Sundance reviews your photos and either keeps them on file for future consideration or discards them. If Sundance selects your jewelry, you will receive a telephone call. Please be advised that Sundance does not return unsolicited samples.

Selling on eBay

Although it's still the king of auction sites, since eBay struck its deal with Buy.com, many smaller sellers have noticed a drop in sales. Since Buy.com added more than five million fixed-price listings to eBay in 2008, it's easy to see how there would be some blow-back affecting auction sales.

The following are some important points to consider if you plan to register as an eBay seller. Actually, these items are important to consider with any product sale.

Image

Buyers will gauge your professional attitude by the quality of your product image. This, when combined with a clear and well-thought-out description of your piece of jewelry, can go far in establishing your potential customer's confidence in you, the seller.

Copy

It's important to write both compelling and legally correct descriptions of your product. Here are some main points to consider:

- Keep in mind the FTC guidelines.
- Provide as much detail about the jewelry as possible. If it includes gemstones, include the country of origin.
- Describe the physical appearance of the jewelry using terms such as *gorgeous, lustrous,* and *classic.*
- Educate your customers about the jewelry making technique used and specific care instructions.
- Carefully check all spelling and punctuation.
- Do not refer to your jewelry as "Yurman-inspired" (or any other designer, for that matter); eBay's published rule is that these types of comparisons are illegal.

Monitor Your Auctions

While your auction is ongoing, potential customers may send you e-mail asking for more information. A good seller keeps on top of these requests and responds in a prompt and courteous fashion.

If your auction is approaching the expiration date and you've received no bids, consider amending your item description. You might also consider promoting your ad using eBay's upgrades. These include opting for inclusion in the eBay Gallery or being featured on the eBay home page rotating Featured Items box.

Feedback

Potential customers will check out your buyers' feedback and read individual comments left by the buyers to gauge whether or not they want to do business with you. When considering the feedback, remember: This is not like school; anything less than an A+ (97 and above) is considered a failing grade in the world of online auctions.

Customer Relations

Like sellers, buyers also have feedback ratings given to them by eBay merchants. To nip potential customer problems in the bud, consider blocking bids from certain customers using your eBay preferences option. A customer may occasionally have negative feedback from sellers when a deal goes south. This is not a reason to carte blanche block their bids. It could be the dispute was the fault of deceptive practices on the part of the seller.

Examples of customers who potentially need blocking are those with Unpaid Items strikes against them, those with feedback in the negative (more negative than positive feedback), or those located in certain countries. Due to rampant credit card fraud in some areas of the world, at present I would only consider shipping to customers in the United States, Canada, and the UK.

Selling on Amazon.com

It used to be that amazon.com was very restrictive in the product categories open to small business. Jewelry is now an available category. However, it is one of the nine categories requiring Amazon approval. Amazon asks that you submit a form with basic company information. They'll evaluate your request and contact you with a decision. The monthly subscription fee is $39.95. Amazon collects a 20 percent referral fee on jewelry sales.

How to Pack Jewelry for Shipping

Both appearance and substance is important when packing jewelry for shipping. Keep your customers happy by having their purchase arrive intact and in packaging suitable for gift giving. Always keep in mind that your customer is buying not only the product but also your wrapping.

For many customers, unwrapping the purchase is part of the thrill of buying. Regardless of the price of the jewelry, I always at least wrap my customer's purchase in attractive coordinated tissue paper with a fabric bow. It's a nice touch to place the jewelry in a velvet drawstring bag. While many will throw a jewelry display box away because it takes up too much space, most will save a velvet drawstring bag to use for other purposes. And, guess what! Each time they use it they will be reminded of your company.

Avoiding Tangling Chains

Place chained necklaces and bracelets on a stiff slotted display board with the chain equally divided so that half lays flat on the front and half lays flat on the back. To further secure the chain, enclose the jewelry in a suitably sized plastic bag. If the bag is too large, fold it to fit and secure it with a piece of clear tape. I also place an anti-tarnish strip in the bag with all my sterling silver jewelry. Take the same precautions with your earrings. Place them on a rigid display with two holes to insert the posts.

Packing Material

Depending on what I'm shipping, I'll use a variety of different packing material. If the jewelry is extremely fragile, I'll encase it in bubble wrap. Otherwise, I cushion the jewelry with recycled shredded paper.

Boxes versus Padded Envelopes

If sending an order via UPS or FedEx expedited delivery, use one of their free padded envelopes or boxes. USPS provides the same type of complimentary shipping material.

I'm partial to boxes simply because they are sturdier. However, if you're shipping a flat necklace or bracelet, a padded envelope will suffice. Ship using the smallest appropriate container; you'll save money on shipping, and your customer will thank you, since many have mail slots with limited clearance.

Delivery Confirmation and Insurance

Delivery confirmation and insurance are a good idea if you are shipping an expensive piece of jewelry to a new customer. I've never had a customer not receive my shipment or receive a damaged package. That being said, I still utilize both extra services occasionally. It's better to spend a bit more on shipping than worry about the lost revenue if a package is lost or your customer denies receiving the package.

At this point, I have covered the nuts and bolts of converting your hobby to a business and getting your home-based jewelry making business up and running. In the last two chapters of the book, we'll explore how to take your jewelry making business to the next level. It's always helpful to look ahead and consider your long-range plans and goals.

12

Take Your Jewelry Making Business to the Next Level

There are two fundamental ways to move your existing business to the next level: mass production of jewelry, and expansion into jewelry-related fields.

Mass Production and Wholesaling

Some jewelry artists are content making individual pieces of jewelry, advancing their skills and reputation to the point where an individual piece of jewelry is set at an expensive price point. Other jewelry artists see an opportunity to increase sales by taking the detailed handcrafted aspect out of the design and turning the operation into a production line.

There isn't a right or a wrong way to go on this. Both approaches can be wildly successful. What matters is determining what's right for you. Down the line, you may even decide to brand under two labels—one for your expensive, handcrafted pieces, and the other for your less-expensive, production-line jewelry.

Quality-Control Issues

When the fabrication of the jewelry is taken out of your immediate control, it is important to monitor your quality control very closely. For example, if you are sending blanks to a casting company for reproduction, it's important that the blank be perfect and the product from the casting company be checked each time your order comes in to make sure the design stays true to the original.

Effective Ordering Techniques

Chapter 6 introduces this topic. Remember, if you are mass-producing jewelry, you will also be purchasing your raw materials in volume. Keep track of what sort of discount terms your vendors offer and maximize your use of them.

Eventually you will come up with your own design for a pendant or charm, and instead of fabricating it yourself out of precious metal sheet or clay, you'll have it mass-produced by a casting company.

Sometimes you'll have a graphic artist do a sketch to represent the design; other times you'll make the blank (a prototype) of the design yourself. It's important you supervise the design work from start to finish, making sure the finished product stays true to form.

Likewise, when you reorder, it's important to spot-check the order to make sure you don't have any faulty product. You can send any weird-looking cast back to the company, eliminating the possibility that it may be inadvertently used in a piece of jewelry by the assembler.

Using Fire Mountain Gems as an example, purchasing more than 200 of any faceted gemstone results in a per-unit price much less than if you purchase twenty here and thirty there. They also have an "assortable" policy that allows you to combine different but like items to get your order over the minimum order amount.

Once you start purchasing in volume, you'll usually be assigned a sales rep employed by your vendor to handle your account. Your sales rep will be able to advise you on current specials and discount terms specific to their employer.

Sales Representatives

A rep can be an invaluable asset for your company, as they can reach many more potential buyers than you can alone. In addition, they have the marketing experience to move your potential customer from initial interest through the objection phase to a completed sale.

How to Find a Representative

Word of mouth is always a good way to find a rep. Another jewelry maker who has a jewelry line unlike yours may be willing to make a referral. Some reps advertise in trade magazines. Setting up a table at a trade show is a great way for the reps to find you. Reps attend trade shows on behalf of their existing clients and walk the trade shows looking for new and unrepresented designers.

Contract Terms

Like all business relationships, there has to be a meeting of the minds. Make sure you have a written contract that defines expectations on both sides. One of the more important facets of the contract is how much it will cost, as you need to factor expense into your cost-of-goods-sold equation. A sales representative is paid a percentage on the wholesale amount of the order. This percentage can vary anywhere from 10 percent to 18 percent. Make sure you address in your contract the fact that any subsequent customer returns are charged against future commissions.

Line Sheets

Regardless of whether you are handling mass marketing yourself or you have a rep, you'll need to prepare a line sheet. A line sheet is a document that gives your buyers all the information they could possibly need about your jewelry. At a minimum, your line sheet should contain the following information:

- Professional-quality images of your jewelry printed at 300 dpi on nice stock
- Layout in portrait format
- Your logo and contact information at the top of each page
- Jewelry style numbers to simplify filling out the order form
- Complete description of each piece of jewelry, including metals, gemstones, lengths, and sizes
- Prices and any applicable discount terms
- If seasonal, cut-off dates for ordering
- Minimum order requirements
- Gemstone color card
- Order forms

Samples

Your rep will need jewelry samples that are typical of your line. Well-known manufacturers often require that their reps purchase the samples. As a brand-new business, this may not fly. Just make sure you adequately insure your sample jewelry in case of theft or other loss.

Hiring Artisan and Production-Line Employees

You can't do everything. Once you start producing jewelry in volume, one option is to subcontract the work out to another jewelry making company, which will significantly increase your cost of goods sold. Your other choice is to hire your own employees, which brings its own special issues—hiring, managing, and firing.

Art School Interns

If you live in a city that has an art school, hiring interns recommended by the school usually works out well. Keep in mind that the interns will usually be young; maturity level can be a problem. Plus, your intern will have to arrange your work schedule around their class schedule and will normally only be available to work part-time.

Paying Interns

The school will be your guide in this arena. I disagree with the notion that interns are gaining such invaluable experience working in your business that payment for services rendered is optional. You get what you pay for. Additionally, the seriousness your intern brings to the job site may be impacted by payment terms.

How to Conduct an Interview

If you have ever conducted an interview, you know that it's grueling sitting on either side of the table. I think interviewing potential employees is one of the most unappealing aspects of owning your own business.

Venue

Even if the job location is your home, conduct your interviews at another location. If you don't have a friend whose office you can use for a few hours, rent a temporary location. You don't want strangers knowing where you live.

Employment Application

Regardless of whether the job is to sweep out your shop or fabricate 22K gold jewelry, every potential employee should fill out a job application. This gives you contact information in the event you hire this applicant.

You can sniff out a potential problem employee just by looking at the application. Gaps in employment or job-hopping can be indicative of people just trying to find themselves. While this is not necessarily a bad thing, it can sometimes be a big red flag, often the sign of someone who is disruptive on the job and either quits or is fired with regularity.

If you're serious about making an offer, call at least one of the old employers to get a reference. In today's litigious atmosphere, many employers are reluctant to give much information. I've found it's helpful to ask if they would hire the person again. Hesitation or a flat-out no pretty much tells the tale.

In that case, I would call at least two other ex-employers. The circumstances of the person's termination may have been beyond their control. You would hate to miss out on a good employee because of one vindictive ex-employer.

Conducting the Interview

It's important to listen. See if what the applicant is saying ties into what they've put on their résumé. Give the applicant logical follow-up questions to judge the depth of their knowledge. It's easy to throw out a few superficial statements; what's hard is expanding upon the superficial if you're not sure about the topic.

Many people are nervous during interviews. See if this emotion seems to go to the extreme. Excessive nervousness may indicate that the person is hiding something. Or it could just mean that they really need the job. Use common sense and evaluate body language. Finally, if this person will be working in your home, make sure you do a criminal background check.

Testing Skills
Invite the applicant to bring their portfolio to the interview, but take this at face value. If the applicant is being interviewed for a job stringing beaded necklaces, have them string a short length complete with clasp during the interview. Do the same for any other jewelry making task for which you are hiring. Give the applicants the opportunity to bring their own tools to the interview. They'll be more comfortable working with the familiar and will be able to give you a fair representation of their skills.

Closing the Interview and the Follow-Up
I have conducted many interviews. It is unfair to be dishonest with the applicant about their hiring chances. Don't leave it open-ended. If you think they will not be a good fit, tell them. Thank them for their time and send them on their way. If the applicant makes you uncomfortable, wait to communicate this fact via telephone.

Tell the applicant when you will be making a decision. Follow up with a quick phone call that day. A quick "Thank you for your time; I've selected another applicant for the job" will suffice. There is no need for an extended dialogue. If the applicant gets belligerent, just hang up.

The Art of Firing
This is difficult even with the most obnoxious employee. It is bad when they cry, attempt to negotiate, or get angry. However, if you have done your job correctly, losing their job should not be a surprise to the employee.

Counseling
Even part-time employees should be counseled when they are irking you. As an employer, I am always irritated if an employee consistently shows up late or conducts a running commentary on their personal problems. Address the problems when they occur and document the discussion in writing.

Young adults can be clueless about the fact that showing up five minutes late every day is just as bad as being an hour late. If it's feasible, offer a later start time.

However, keep in mind that it's not your job to rearrange the company structure for an employee's benefit.

The Last Day

It's best to fire a person on a Friday near the end of their workday. The day transitions into a weekend, which they normally have off, so there is less shock. Have their final and complete paycheck ready. Once again, I don't think there is any need for an extended dialogue if you've had prior discussions with the employee about their performance.

It's excruciating watching an employee clean out their work space. During the exit interview, get as many employees as possible into another part of the office. Don't give the exiting employee a chance to start a dialogue with other employees; keep the humiliation factor to a minimum. Make sure you get all keys from the employee. I would change the exterior locks as well, immediately.

Attracting Outside Investors and Maintaining Control

When you are ready to take your business to the next level, you may find you lack adequate financing. You will probably need to rent a facility and purchase expensive jewelry making equipment. Inventory levels will be stepped up. More production means more payroll expenses. While you may have been able to fund your business start-up without borrowing, pushing into mass production may make it a necessity.

I'm not discussing an Initial Public Offering (IPO) in this chapter. This topic is very complex and totally outside the scope of this book. What I do cover are the pros and cons of getting outside investors to help finance your business. If the business does well, they share in the profits. If the business fails, they lose their money. There is the associated issue of loss of control.

Corporations

If your business is a corporation, you accomplish funding with the use of debt or equity.

Equity

The outside investor pays the market rate for shares of your corporate stock. They make money by either selling the shares of stock for more than they paid or by your corporation issuing dividends on earnings.

Debt

The outside investor loans your business money, attaching the prevailing rate of interest on the money. A simple example: If a bank has issued you a line of credit, they are invested in your business.

Partnerships

Investors in partnerships are called partners. They can be passive (doing no work for the partnership) or non-passive (actively involved in the daily operations and decision-making process). New investors/partners are brought in by allocating existing partner shares.

Sole Proprietorships

Since a sole proprietorship has one and only one owner, outside funding comes only from loans to the business.

Advantages and Disadvantages of Having Outside Investors

Advantages

- Extra cash
- Potential additional experience brought in by the investor
- Payments to equity investors are made only when you have the money

Disadvantages

- More voices and more feedback on business decisions
- Loss of control if your ownership goes below 50 percent
- Possible restructuring of the business, making it easier for outside investors to sell their interest (perhaps to individuals you don't want to be doing business with)

Types of Outside Investors

- Family
- Friends

- Business contacts
- Business angels—wealthy individuals who invest money in businesses and typically also offer their business expertise to help build the business

Consider this method of increasing cash flow very carefully. It is a rare person indeed who gives money with no strings attached. Make sure you are happy with the implicit terms that come with the exchange of money. I would always prefer borrowing needed funds from a disinterested third party such as a bank rather than taking in a partner.

Everyone's situation is different. Accepting investors may be perfect for your business—especially if they bring a jewelry making or business talent to the table that you lack.

Expanding Beyond the Jewelry Making Business

Read the biographies of any of your favorite designers, jewelry or otherwise, and you will see that many expand outside their original area of design. Alexander Calder, the great American artist and sculptor, is best known for creating the mobile. However, Calder also created many pieces of stunning hammered metal and gemstone jewelry. The influence of his sculpturing background showed in his jewelry, and vice versa.

David Yurman originally studied sculpture and came into the jewelry-design business after a short career as sculptor. After positive reaction to an angel-shaped copper belt buckle that he designed for his wife, Sybil, Yurman started experimenting with wire jewelry. This led to his signature twisted helix design. Costume jewelry giant Monet started in 1937 as an offshoot of a company that produced metal art deco monograms for purses. Rhode Island School of Design graduate Kenneth Jay Lane designed shoes before starting his forty-year-old jewelry empire.

The point of all this: It is entirely possible and most probably profitable to design across product lines. Take your jewelry making skills and apply them to a complementary industry.

Expand by Tracking Fashion Trends

Jeweled Garments

Jeweled garments are a strong possible area of expansion. Evening and bridal wear has always had elements of jewelling. Clothing designer Vera Wang brought jeweled garments into daywear, a trend that doesn't seem to be slowing down. This is a logical expansion for a jewelry making business.

The clothing designs are very simple in nature to offset the elaborateness of the jeweled embellishment. So no real clothing design experience is needed, just access to wholesale gemstones and crystals. Fabrication of the garments could be subcontracted out, with the final design work on the finished garment done in-house.

Jeweled Handbags

The queen of jeweled handbags is Judith Leiber. The use of crystals and beading to embellish her handbags is her signature style. Simple clutch handbags with drawstring openings are extremely easy to design and make. Purchase luxury materials such as velvet and butter-soft suede in volume, have the handbags sewn, then bead them in-house. For some inspiration, check out Leiber's awesome designs at www.judithleiber.com.

Accessories for the Home

This is a particularly logical spin-off for metalworkers. The possibilities for metal switch plates, wall decorations, and light fixtures are endless. The same hammering techniques used to forge metal into jewelry are applicable for creating sculptural works of art.

Set crystals in grout for a decorative edge similar to tile. Tumbled crystals purchased by the pound are extremely inexpensive yet add a luxe touch to trim. The crystals could be set alternating with recycled glass tiles in a bath or kitchen. This is not a hard skill to master. You could form a completely different business unit around the home renovation and decorating industry.

Transforming Jewelry

Looking at some of Alexander Calder's metalwork necklaces or Peter Chang's resin brooches, it is easy to see how these are actually transformable jewelry—suitable for both street wear and for hanging on the wall of a home.

An excellent book to reference on the topic of transforming jewelry is *Sculpture to Wear: The Jewelry of Marjorie Schick* by Tacey Rosolowski.

Other Ideas

In closing, think about making metal- and gemstone-decorated greeting cards, stringing crystals or gemstones on knitting yarn, or using wire-wrapping techniques to create Christmas tree decorations. The possibilities are endless.

Part of your master plan to move your home-based jewelry making business to the next level may call for training and certification. The last chapter of this book gives information on these topics, along with various jewelry industry trade organizations.

13

Jewelry Making Training and Certification

I highly recommend joining trade organizations. They provide not only the opportunity to network with your peers but also to keep current with jewelry making education and events. In addition, membership also includes the ability to participate in group discounts.

Jewelry Making Trade Organizations

American Craft Council

Members of American Craft Council, a nonprofit educational organization, receive *American Craft*, the best magazine available in the United States about the arts and crafts industry. *American Craft* covers many important noncreative-type issues, such as how to get affordable health insurance, preparing for juried shows, and photography guides for great images.

The magazine alone is worth the price of membership. At publication date the membership dues are $40 per year, $55 if you live outside the United States. Other benefits include free entry to various council arts and crafts shows and access to the American Craft Council's impressive reference library located in New York City. Visit www.craftcouncil.org for more information.

Society of North American Goldsmiths (SNAG)

Everyone who works with metal, whether it's gold or other metals, should consider a SNAG membership. SNAG has yearly conferences providing access to some of the premier metalworkers in the United States. They also have a newsletter containing invaluable resources on marketing your work, various grants available, and continuing education opportunities.

A complimentary subscription to *Metalsmith* magazine is included with your membership. While *American Craft* is very practical, *Metalsmith* is what I call a coffee-table magazine. The photography is stunning. I never read an issue without feeling an instant infusion of creativity. Learn more at www.snagmetalsmith.org.

Society of American Silversmiths (SAS)

If you are in the business of working with sterling silver, this is the organization for you. The Society provides invaluable information on creating and caring for sterling silver objects. One recent educational topic was how to use three-inch sterling silver discs to form small vessels, lidded containers, or seamless tubes to slice and form finger rings. Visit www.silversmithing.com for more information.

Manufacturing Jewelers and Suppliers of America (MJSA)

In addition, check out membership in MJSA (www.mjsa.org). Some membership advantages include group discounts on insurance, booth discounts at MJSA Expo New York, and buyers' guides and referrals.

Jewelry Making Certifications

If you have jewelry making certification, make sure to add it to your résumé.

Jewelers of America Bench Certification

This certification rates jewelers according to nationally recognized standards. Among bench jewelers it has the same cache as being a CPA does with accountants or passing the bar exam for attorneys. To gain certification you must pass both a written and a hands-on skills test. An applicant can achieve certification in four different areas:

- Certified Bench Jeweler Technician
- Certified Bench Jeweler
- Certified Senior Bench Jeweler
- Certified Master Bench Jeweler

Find out more about these certifications by visiting the Jewelers of America Web site at www.jewelers.org. In the site search box, type *professional development* to access the exact page.

Art Clay Certification

For those working with precious metal clay, certification is also available. Those passing the test are able to purchase Art Clay products at a 35 percent discount at online jewelry supplier Rio Grande (a pretty strong incentive to be certified) and are able to teach Art Clay classes.

The certification involves making several pieces of Art Clay jewelry incorporating items such as cork, porcelain, and fused-glass cabochons. You'll then have to use various methods to fabricate pendants, rings, and earrings. The use of a variety of different tools is also mandatory.

For more information about this certification, contact the Precious Metal Clay Guild (PMCG) at www.pmcguild.com. The Web site also contains many interesting links that provide more information about working with precious metal clay. The Mitsubishi Corporation founded PMCG in 1997. One of the corporate divisions manufactures precious metal clay.

One fact to keep in mind regarding certification: Many times certification takes a backseat to entry into juried shows, awards, and press in the eyes of your customers. Does that mean being certified is not an avenue to pursue? Depending on your jewelry making specialty, being certified is extremely worthwhile as your company gains respect among your peers and potential wholesalers.

Universities and Colleges Offering Related Degrees

Rhode Island School of Design (RISD)

RISD is a very prestigious four-year university offering degrees in the fields of art and design. For those interested in jewelry making, they have a fantastic program in jewelry and metalsmithing. The program includes fabrication, the history of adornment, color technique, and using alternative methods.

If you live in the area but don't have the time to pursue a degree, they also offer interesting continuing education classes for an extremely reasonable price. One of my favorites is The History of Costume Jewelry, which only costs $150. There are also technical continuing education classes covering metal casting and materials. A great class that is available online is Build Your Online Portfolio. For more information about RISD, visit their Web site at www.risd.edu.

Kendall College of Art and Design

This college, located in Grand Rapids, Michigan, offers a bachelor's degree in fine arts (BFA) in metals and jewelry design. Students learn about the history of metalworking and study traditional as well as technology-based methods. Besides traditional metals, you'll also be working with stainless steel and plastics. They also offer an interesting CAD/CAM class. For more information, visit their Web site at www.kcad.edu.

Savannah College of Art and Design

Located in historic downtown Savannah, Georgia, this school also offers a BFA in metals and jewelry design. You'll prepare for a career in industrial, fine arts, or small-business settings, studying traditional jewelry, metalsmithing, and silversmithing techniques. One of their visiting artists is Komelia Okim, pioneer of the Kum-Boo Technique. For more information, visit their Web site at www.scad.edu.

Complete List of Colleges and Universities

For a complete list of colleges and universities offering jewelry and metalsmithing classes, visit SNAG's Web site. The address is www.snagmetalsmith.org. On the top toolbar, select *Programs/Resources > Educational Institutions*. From there, open the Excel file (sort by state, a data sort for the E column).

Weeklong Seminars at Regional Arts and Crafts Schools

American Craft and *Metalsmith* magazines always have advertisements for regional schools that offer intense one- and two-week seminars on different jewelry making techniques. Many times they are set up like universities, with the students living on campus with 24/7 access to the workroom. You may have a school in your local area. If not, consider the value of traveling to one to advance your jewelry making skills.

Flipping through my recent edition of *American Craft*, one example I found is the Haystack Mountain School of Crafts (www.haystack-mtn.org), located in Deer Isle, Maine. They offer weeklong classes in bead making (a logical next step for beaders wishing to expand their design style), enamels, precious metal clay, and fabrication.

If you would like to find schools in your local area, do a Google search using the key phrase "arts and crafts schools in [your state name]."

Local Trade Schools and Teaching Museums

Even if you aren't lucky enough to live near an arts and crafts school, you probably have a trade school in your area offering jewelry and metalsmithing classes at night. I've gotten many positive reviews from friends who have taken such classes.

There is usually a very hands-on rather than textbook-oriented approach to learning the skills. If you're not an intense type of learner, trade school classes will be very appropriate for you. They normally take place for a few hours one or two nights a week for two or three months, like regular university classes.

I've also had the opportunity to take jewelry making classes at a local teaching museum. These classes usually take place on a Saturday or Sunday in three- or four-hour sessions. The classes will normally consist of eight classes, spanning a period of two months.

Just one bit of advice about taking classes at a teaching museum: Most of the instructors are required to give classes in exchange for free studio space. I have had very dedicated instructors and instructors who sat in the back of the workroom eating, irritated if you disturbed them or didn't catch on to the technique quickly enough.

My best advice if you are signing up for any type of course that involves a significant amount of investment—whether it's time or money—on your part is to speak with past students. Tracking down old students may not be feasible. A backup plan is to check with the particular school or museum's policy on refunds (although I've found that most will not give a refund under any condition).

In Conclusion

If I had to emphasize just one aspect of starting a new business, it would be that you need to go into this with serious intent, or keep your jewelry making at the hobby level. Remember, even a part-time business needs to be no-nonsense. To operate otherwise would be a waste of your valuable time and money.

Second, there will be days when you feel that it's just not going to work out. I've been there many times. Push past that phase. Explore new outlets to market your jewelry. Don't be discouraged if you hear the word *no* a lot. You probably will. I was turned down for the first few juried events I entered. However, I kept on trying until I was finally successful.

Occasionally, you'll need to take a step back and evaluate the way you are running your business. Is it working? If not, revise your business plan. Constantly work to hone your jewelry making skills. Down the line, you will be glad you did. Skim every magazine you can get your hands on. I've found good marketing and business management ideas in the weirdest places. With hard work and determination, your business will be a success. I did it. You can too!

Source Directory

Web-Based Suppliers

C.C. Silver and Gold Sheet

2028 West Camelback
Phoenix, AZ 85015
Customer Service: (602) 242-6310
Fax: (602) 433-9522
www.ccsilver.com

Contenti Jewelry Supplies & Tools

515 Narragansett Park Drive
Pawtucket, RI 02861
Customer Service: (401) 305-3000
Fax: (800) 651-1887
www.contenti.com

The Earth Bazaar Gemstones

56 Newtown Turnpike
Westport, CT 06880
Customer Service: (800) 424-5149
www.theearthbazaar.com

EE Beads Jewelry making Kits

P.O. Box 10
Willow Grove, PA 19090-0010
Customer Service: (215) 658-1711

Fax: (215) 658-1191

www.eebeads.com/_kits.htm

Fire Mountain Gems and Beads

One Fire Mountain Way

Grants Pass, OR 97526-2373

Customer Service: (800) 423-2319

Order by Phone: (800) 355-2137

Order by Fax: (800) 292-3473

www.firemountaingems.com

Grassman-Blake Quality Clasps

58 East Willow Street

Millburn, NJ 07041

Customer Service: (800) 537-6370

Fax: (800) 842-2881

www.gbclasp.com

Hong Kong Lapidaries—Wholesale Faceted Gemstones and Beads

2801 University Drive

Coral Springs, FL 33065

Customer Service: (954) 755-8777

Fax: (954) 755-8780

www.hklap.com

House of Gems—Wholesale Beads & Jewelry Making Supplies

607 South Hill Street

Los Angeles, CA 90014

Customer Service: (877) 436-7123

Fax: (877) 436-7112

www.houseofgems.com

Jamming Gems

Customer Service: (800) 903-4367

www.jamminggems.com

JewelrySupply.com—Complete Line of Supplies and Tools

Customer Service: (866) 380-7464

Fax: (916) 780-9617

www.jewelrysupply.com

Match Pair—Matching Gemstone Sets

10845 North Coyote Lane

Tucson, AZ 85742

Customer Service: (520) 818-8206

www.matchpair.com

Opal Trader

P.O. Box 49

Old Noarlunga, 5168

South Australia, Australia

http://opal-trader.com

Ortery Photosimile Digital Image Light Box

8 Hammond Drive, Suite 112

Irvine, CA 92618

www.ortery.com/technology/about_photosimile_lightbox_technology.php

Otto Frei Jewelry Tools, Supplies, and Findings

126 Second Street

Oakland, California 94607

Customer Service: (800) 772-3456

www.ottofrei.com

Pasternak Jewelry Findings and Supplies

P.O. Box 4767

Tel-Aviv 61047

Israel

U.S. Customer Service: (866) 450-7774

www.pasternakfindings.com

Pehnec Lab-Created Gemstones

P.O. Box 1038
Garden Grove, CA 92842
Customer Service: (714) 537-0473
www.pehnec.com

Rio Grande Jewelry Supplies and Tools

P.O. Box 12277
Albuquerque, NM 87195
Order by Phone: (800) 545-6566
www.riogrande.com

Rishashay Fine Sterling Silver Beads

P.O. Box 8271
Missoula, MT 59807
Customer Service: (800) 517-3311
Fax: (800) 549-3467
www.rishashay.com

Table Top Studio—Digital Image Light Tents

4187 Carpineria Avenue #11
Carpineria, CA 93013
http://www.tabletopstudio.com

Topearl—Loose Akoya, Freshwater, and Tahitian Pearls

No. 11-12C, Ground Floor
Liwan Plaza
Kangwang South Road
Guangzhous, China 510140
http://www.topearl.com/wholesale.php/4

Tripps Jewelry Making Supplies and Kits

P.O. Box 1369
Socorro, NM 87801
Customer Service: (800) 545-7962

Fax: (505) 835-2848

www.tripps.com

Via Murano—Venetian Beads, Tornado Crimps, and
Snapeez Jump Rings
17664 Newhope Street, Suite A
Fountain Valley, CA 92708
Customer Service: (714) 708-2687
www.viamurano.com

Trade Organizations

American Craft Council
72 Spring Street
New York, NY 10012-4019
(212) 274-0630
Fax: (212) 274-0650
www.craftcouncil.org

Manufacturing Jewelers and Suppliers of America (MJSA)
45 Royal Little Drive
Providence, RI 02904
(401) 274-3840
www.mjsa.org

Society of American Silversmiths (SAS)
P.O. Box 72839
Providence, RI 02907
(401) 461-6840
Fax: (401) 461-6841
www.silversmithing.com

Society of North American Goldsmiths (SNAG)
540 Oak Street, Suite A
Eugene, OR 97401

(541) 345-5689
Fax: (541) 345-1123
www.snagmetalsmith.org

Jewelry-Related Shows

American Craft Council
Holds six public shows each year in the following cities: Baltimore, Maryland; Atlanta, Georgia; St. Paul, Minnesota; San Francisco, California; Charlotte, North Carolina; and Sarasota, Florida.
www.craftcouncil.org

Couture Jewelry Trade Show
If you fabricate high-end jewelry, don't miss the Couture show. It takes place every year in May or June at the Wynn, Las Vegas, Nevada, and is attended by retailers with jewelry stores. Exhibitors must pass a rigorous juried process.
www.couturejeweler.com

Craft Organization Development Association (CODA)
Held yearly in different parts of the United States, the CODA conference gives information about CraftNet, an alliance of technical schools with arts and crafts programs and best-practices presentations.
P.O. Box 51
Onia, AR 72663
(870) 746-5159
www.codacraft.org

Jewelers of America New York Trade Shows
Given three times a year (spring, fall, and winter), this show provides the opportunity to meet face to face with jewelry buyers from across the United States.
52 Vanderbilt Ave, 19th Floor
New York, NY 10017
(800) 223-0673
www.ja-newyork.com

Manufacturing Jewelers and Suppliers of America (MJSA) Expo New York

For those in the jewelry manufacturing business, this show provides a look at the latest machines, supplies, and services. It's held in New York, New York, in the spring of each year at the Jacob Javits Convention Center.

(800) 444-6572

www.mjsatradeshows.org/expoNY.php

Manufacturing Jewelers and Suppliers of America (MJSA) Trade Show for Jewelry Making

This trade show gives jewelry makers a chance to see a full range of industry-related products, including beads, tools, packaging and displays, gemstones, and pearls. It's offered in the fall in various locations throughout northeastern United States.

www.mjsatradeshows.org/tradeshowjewelrymaking.php

Society of North American Goldsmiths (SNAG)

SNAG holds its yearly educational conference each year in May/June at various locations in the United States. You'll have a chance to attend hands-on jewelry making classes and other business-related seminars.

www.snagmetalsmith.org

Tucson Gem Show

The premier yearly show for those interested in buying gems, minerals, and fossils, it's given in the spring of each year at various locations in Tucson, Arizona.

www.tucsonshowguide.com

Women's Jewelry Association

This association sponsors yearly events such as Women in the Know and the Awards for Excellence Gala.

7000 West Southwest Highway

Chicago Ridge, IL 60415

(708) 361-6266

womensjewelryassociation.com

Educational Resources

About.com Jewelry Making

Follow guide Tammy Powley as she walks you through the basics of several jewelry making techniques, including beading, wirework, and soldering.
jewelrymaking.about.com

Adobe Line Sheets: Layers—The How-to Magazine for Adobe

If you use Adobe to create your line sheets, here are some instructions on how to modify them for changes.
www.layersmagazine.com/designers-revamp-a-jewelry-artists-line-sheet.html

Arrowmont School of Arts and Crafts

Arrowmont provides classes on many different jewelry making techniques, from soldering to making glass beads.
556 Parkway
Gaitlinburg, TN 37738
(865) 436-5860
www.arrowmont.org

ArtMetal

ArtMetal is a social networking site for metalworking jewelers providing instructions and tips. In the site search box, enter the technique or skill you would like to learn more about. To get a generic set of instructions, just type *Instructions* into the site search box.
www.artmetal.com

Beading FAQ by Swallow Hill Creations

Beaders will appreciate these practical tips, such as how to keep beads from jumping around while you are working with them and how to get loose beads on working thread.
www.swallowhillcreations.com/FAQ.htm

Bellaonline.com—Jewelry making Tips

Follow editor Debbie Witenski as she walks you through many basic jewelry making techniques, such as beading, wirework, and soldering.

www.bellaonline.com/site/JewelryMaking

Color Marketing

Before you buy gemstones, go to this site to learn more about the latest color and design trends.

www.colormarketing.org

The Crafts Report

The business resource for artists and retailers.

www.craftsreport.com

The Crucible

A nonprofit educational facility teaching the basic skills needed to work with precious metals, set stones, and create jewelry. You'll also learn how to apply these techniques to making candlesticks and sculptures.

1260 Seventh Street

Oakland, CA 94607

(510) 444-0918

www.thecrucible.org

EZcube® Light Box

These detailed instructions on how to take digital images using the EZcube will be helpful even if you don't own one.

www.ezcube.com/step-by-step.html

Fire Mountain Gems and Beads

In addition to being a stellar supplier, Fire Mountain's site also includes hundreds of free jewelry making patterns and instructions. Go to the Web site and select *Beading Instructions* on the top toolbar.

www.firemountaingems.com

The Ganoksin Project
A fantastic free online resource for and by jewelers, providing jewelry making technical and educational articles and tips.
www.ganoksin.com

JagWear
Learn how to make your own wire-wrapping jig.
www.jagwearjewelry.com/wirejig.htm

Jewelry Making @ Bloglander
A great free source of jewelry making news, tips, and tutorials for and by other jewelry makers.
www.bloglander.com/jewelrymaking/category/jewelry

Lapidary Art—Basic Jewelry Photography
Easy-to-understand instructions for those using a 35mm camera.
www.lapidaryart.com/projects_2.html

The Lapidary Journal
This print magazine has an online presence providing free metal, bead, and clay jewelry making projects. The site also has a comprehensive listing of free technical projects, such as bezel basics and gem-setting procedures.
www.lapidaryjournal.com

Nourish Your Spirit Gold-Filled Earring Instructions
Perfect your forging and metalworking skills with these easy instructions to make a pair of African hammered gold earrings. No soldering required.
www.nourish-your-spirit.com/african_earrings.html

Resizing Images for your Web Site
Easy-to-understand ABCs of resizing high-res images to 72 ppi—the correct file size for the Internet.
www.jewelrymakinghq.com/resize_pictures_website.htm

SNAG

SNAG publishes a complete list of colleges and universities offering jewelry and metalworking classes. Go to SNAG's Web site, and on the top toolbar, select *Programs/Resources > Educational Institutions.*
www.snagmetalsmith.org

Starving Jewelry Artists Forum

Dedicated to giving jewelry designers a place to learn, grow, inspire, and be inspired.
www.starvingjewelryartists.com

Sunshine Artist

This site keeps you updated on all the latest arts and crafts shows accepting entries. The Sunshine forum is a valuable source of information as to which shows to attend and which to avoid.
www.sunshineartist.com

Via Murano Wire-Wrapping Tips

Detailed instructions with clear explanatory images on how to wire-wrap loops.
www.viamurano.com/store/pc/viewcontent.asp?idpage=15

WebPhotoSchool.com

Easy-to-understand instructions for those using a digital camera.
www.olympusamerica.com/cpg_section/lessons/vault/index.html

Acknowledgments

"To the Ursuline nuns and Jesuit priests who provided me with a stellar education, and my parents who selflessly footed the bill.

To my agent Barb Doyen for all her hard work and support.

And to Ellen Urban for her months of editing, follow through and advice."

Index

certifications, 189–90
software, 38–40
techniques, 25–29
trade organizations, 188–89
jewelry shows, in-home, 143–44
Juried Art Services, 147

karated gold, 134–35
Kendall College of Art and Design, 191
knock-offs, 129–30

lab-created gemstones, 138
label-maker software, 37
Lane, Kenneth Jay, 23–24
layaway, 149
lead, 138
left-brain characteristics, 10, 11
legal and ethical issues, 125–38
Legal Match, 129
Leiber, Judith, 186
letterhead, 77
licensing, 128–29
light diffusers, 45–47
lighting, 44, 163
limited runs, 19–20
line sheets, 179
logos, 76–77
Lookbook, The, 152
Luxe MG, 153

magnifiers, 44
manual bookkeeping, 110–11
Manufacturing Jewelers and Suppliers of
    America (MJSA), 189
marketing, 139–53, 171–72
marketing plans, 58, 64–65
mass production and wholesaling, 177–80
metal scraps, 49
Metalsmith magazine, 21, 189
Microsoft Office Accounting Professional, 37, 111

Microsoft Office FrontPage, 154–55
Microsoft Office templates, 37
Monet, 23
moonlighting, 17, 18
Morris, Robert Lee, 55
museums, 144, 192

net income, 116, 119
niche, establishing, 4
Nourish Your Spirit, 138

office, setting up, 33–42
office supplies, 34–35, 36
ombre effect, 48
Orchid Boutique, 13
Ortery Photosimile Light Box, 46–47
ownership types, 55–58

packing jewelry for shipping, 175–76
Parmalee, Anna, 186
partnerships, 184
part-time work, 17, 18
past-due accounts, 107–8
payment processors, 159
PayPal, 43, 72–73, 159
Peachtree software, 38
pearls, 95, 136–37
Peretti, Elsa, 125
persistence, 4–5
photographic equipment, 45–48
photography, digital, 39–40, 47, 162–63
pinging, 169
pitch ideas, 180
pitch letters, 139
plan of operations, 58–59, 65
plated gold, 135
platinum, 135
polymer clay, 26
postcards, 78
precious metal clay, 25–26

About the Author

Maire Loughran, who built her jewelry-making business from the ground floor up, writes and lectures on the topic of how to start a home-based business. She also acts as a mentor to other new, jewelry-making business startups. Maire is a member of the American Craft Council, Society of American Silversmiths, and the Society of North American Goldsmiths. In addition, she is the Arts/Crafts Business Guide at About.com and the Feature Jewelry Writer at Suite101.com.